AFFLUVIA

The toxic off-gassing of affluent culture

Johanna Drucker

Copyright © 2025 Johanna Drucker and Bridge Books
All Rights Reserved

Published by Bridge Books, 2858 W. Belle Plaine Ave., #3, Chicago, IL, U.S.A
bridge-books.org

ISBN: 979-8-9879330-8-4

Library of Congress CIP #: 2025933521

Cover Image: Johanna Drucker.

Notes on production: All paintings and diagrams are by the author.

Cover and interior design by Michael Workman Studio.

This book was typeset using Adobe Caslon Pro, Filosophia OT, Park Lane and Source Sans Pro typefaces and is printed on acid-free paper by Ingram Spark.

CONTENTS

Introduction: Daily Habits	*19*
One: Making coffee	*25*
Two: Feeding the cats	*235*
Afterword: Out the door	*299*

CONTENTS (EXPANDED)

Introduction: Daily Habits	19
Part One: Making Coffee	25
Beans: Many hands	25
Coffee farming: Landscapes & labors	27
Harvesting and Processing: Picky work	35
Sorting: Up in the air	41
Packing and Roasting: Trucks and travels	45
The Bag: Industrial processes of all kinds	51
PET plastic film:	

A massive industry   54

The gas release valve:

   Taking shape(s)   67

Sticky layers: Adhesive   70

Printing: Color for

   the consumer   72

The tin tie: A surprise link

   to hay bales   74

Grinder: Magnetism, motor,

   and real steel   78

The spring: Iron ore

   from the stars   83

Coke production:

   Turning up the heat   88

Steel: Blasting the alloy   93

Emissions and Pollutants:

Trying to come clean	97
The spring: Flexibility under stress	99
Human costs: People in the process	100
The blade: Cold metal, sharp edge	103
Gaskets and rings:	
The soft rubber parts	107
The lid: Hard plastics	112
The motor: From charge to spin	114
Outer casing: The hard shell	120
The power cord:	
The chemical threat	125
Paper filter: From forest to trash	130
Glass Jar for the Beans: Chipped but loyal	142
Glass: Sand to bottle	143
The Cuff: Familiar plastic	152
The Shiny Lid: Another metal	153

Coffee maker: Miracles of circuitry   *160*

  Canister: Insulation mysteries   *161*

  LEDs: Excitation of electrons   *167*

  Digital clock: Backlight and crystal   *172*

  Digital circuits:

    Computers on my counter   *179*

  Batteries: Esoteric toxins   *183*

  The copper heating element:

    Thermal energy and pastes   *185*

Half and half: The animals appear   *194*

  Milk production:

    Hazards in the dairy   *195*

  Manure: Managing methane gas   *202*

  The carton: From flatland

    to container   *204*

Coffee cup: Ceramic durability   *213*

Part Two: Feeding the cats — 235

   The can: Punched and rolled — 235

   The food: Unimaginable ingredients — 239

   The label: Dressing it up — 245

   The bowls: Enduring pyrex — 250

   The cheap spoon: Cut and pressed — 257

   Warmth: (Un)natural gas — 261

   Water: The long journey — 266

      The source: Ongoing conflicts — 268

      Water treatment: From sky to sink — 270

   Waste: More expertise — 280

   Electricity: Those energetic electrons — 288

Afterword: Out the door — 299

Insidious pollution — 304

Conclusion — 311

Endnotes — 315

Introduction: Daily Habits

Every morning, I go into the kitchen, make my coffee, and feed my cats. The familiar routine takes about ten minutes. I get the jar of coffee beans from the fridge, pull out a paper filter, grind my beans, start the brewing, open the can of cat food, scoop it into bowls and so forth almost without pause. By the time I am filling my cup the animals have finished their wet food and are crunching their dry kibble. The activity takes no effort, no conscious reflection. The actions proceed automatically while I think about the day ahead.

After coffee, I set out for a daily jog through my quiet neighborhood on the Westside of Los Angeles. Traffic sounds are always part of the background. The low roar of the freeway is like that of a distant river. Each day is slightly different. I sense the mood of the early morning while watching the sun's slow rise above the mountains to the East. The residential streets are quiet except for the occasional hiss of automatic sprinklers.

Mine is a modest-seeming existence. My lifestyle is undistinguished in terms of consumption. I drive a gasoline-powered car more than a decade old that has very low mileage. I live in a wood-frame, 1950s-era, cottage-bungalow with a drought-tolerant yard I take care of myself. My near-empty recycling and trash bins would hardly merit weekly pick-up except for the rapid decay of food waste in the warm climate. In comparison with that of my neighbors, my carbon footprint is small.

Or is it?

Finding the answer to that question took me on a dizzying series of investigations. This book is the result of exploring the connections between that ten-minute morning routine and the multiple systems of extraction, human exploitation, and natural resource destruction on which it depends. Not only does my lifestyle pollute, but the more I researched, the more I discovered about the complicated relations between these mundane daily activities and lifecycles of production and destruction to which I am usually oblivious.

Let's revisit those morning routines—I make coffee and feed the cats—in a bit more detail.

I go into the kitchen and flip on the light, take a glass jar of coffee beans from the fridge. Nearly empty, it needs to be refilled from the bag in the freezer. The moisture-proof bag is coated with a skin of ink in organic shades of green, brown, and orange. I remove an unbleached paper filter from a carton

Introduction: Daily Habits

in the drawer under the counter and fit it into the cone of the electric coffee maker. I twist off the top of the aluminum coffee canister, run water into it and pour this into the reservoir, gauging the level through a transparent plastic window marked in cup measures. The coffee beans, sweet smelling and pungent, slide into the electric grinder and I press on the lid. The electrical circuit completes, the blade spins and whirs, the sound shifts from high pitched cracking to a smooth purr as the beans are pulverized to powder. I knock the fresh grounds into the filter, snap the coffee-maker lid closed, and hit the buttons on the front of the console. Blue LED lights glow as the water begins to be heated by an electrical element I can't see, though I hear the gurgle and hissing it produces. The LCD panel shows me the time.

From another cabinet, I take out a can of cat food. The felines prowl, eager and attentive. My finger slips through the ring of the pop-top on the can, and I pull against the smooth curl of metal as the sharp edge of the lid separates from the rim. Inside, gleaming wet, the brown paté shines as it exudes an odor that appeals to the animals. I pick up a small metal spoon and scoop the food into their bowls, smashing it into small clumps that are easier for them to pick up in their jaws. In a few minutes, as they finish their first course and I am pouring my coffee and adding a touch of half-and-half from a waxed paper carton, I will give them a handful of dry food. I settle down to my desk and the day has begun as usual.

=

The coffee gets made and the cats get fed.... Just that. Those two small actions, so familiar that they hardly register as having any ecological consequences, are the full subject of this account. Why? Because as soon as they are examined in detail, they lead through multifarious connections to incredibly complex systems. I am confronted with the reality that my modest-seeming lifestyle is anything but. By examining a single, simple, morning routine that takes barely ten minutes I became aware of the fact that every act, no matter how insignificant or banal, is embedded in a global network of interconnections and consequences.

As I realize what is involved in making coffee and feeding the cats, I wonder how I can go on doing this, given the impacts, unless radical changes can be effected. What level of denial am I practicing? Even my modest lifestyle is exhaling vast amounts of toxic flatulence into the atmosphere, contributing steadily to the greenhouse gases suffocating our world and creating conditions of vast social inequality.

Affluvia is the term I use to describe this toxic off-gassing. Literally, this means the emissions, gases, and pollution generated by affluence. Affluence is a condition of existence lived well-above the levels of subsistence, buffered with excess, but which passes in our first-world privilege as modest and unremarkable. The term affluvia is meant to be suggestive, with a metaphoric aspect that invokes the image of toxins exuded into the social atmospheres and cultural ecosystems we inhabit as well as the physical world. How oblivious can we be for how long?

What, if anything, would or could alter my—our—dependence on the global networks and systems of production that sustain our complicity? To answer, I set out to discover the invisible underpinnings of my morning routine. Resources for research are abundant. Answers to the existential questions are not. My research does not lead me to solutions, only a deeper understanding of my own relation to the world.

Part One: Making Coffee

Begin with the coffee… Each step of this process—the beans, the grinder, the coffee maker, a paper filter, the half and half, my coffee cup, and other parts of the routine—turns out to be a part of vast production networks when subjected to focused investigation.

● ●

The Coffee Beans: Many hands
As I begin my research, I wonder how many hands my beans have passed through to reach mine?

The beans are deep brown-black with a fine sheen. They tumble in a narrow stream with a light clicking sound as their hulls rub against each other. This is the end of their long journey–from where? A field or a mountainside? In South or Central America? The package identifies them as "Arabica" from multiple sources. I quickly find out that the source must lie in the band between 30 degrees south and 28 degrees north of the Equator. This is known as the "coffee belt." This band circles the globe and includes radically different territories (and working conditions) from Yemen to Brazil, Central America and Vietnam, India and the Caribbean, as well as parts of Africa and Indonesia.

My detective work pauses for a momentary detour into history. I find that the first documented occurrence of cultivated coffee is in 13th century Yemen and Ethiopia. It was introduced to Europe by way of Italy in the 16th century, though, again, never grown on that continent. When coffee houses opened in Europe, they produced a plague of jabbering chatter as over-stimulated drinkers responded to the caffeine–and were caricatured in printed broadsides. Newspapers and chocolate were also part of the heady mix, and the resulting effect on persons previously accustomed to drinking beer and other fermented beverages is well-documented in humorous accounts of the period. Boozy moods gave way to boisterous, hyper-active conversational exchange. Some scholars have suggested that caffeine had profound cultural impacts—including fomenting revolutionary ideas in politics, science, and other domains because of its properties as a stimulant. Now it is simply a readily available morning drink, like mine.

Back to tracking my beans, I now realize coffee is not grown in California, or in North America or Europe. We don't have the climate for it. So no matter where they grow, the bright cherries, as they are called, are from places far from my kitchen, raised in communities to which I have no direct connection, cultivated and harvested by people I will never know.

Coffee farming: Landscapes and labors
As I gently tap the beans into place in the shining metal well of the grinder with my finger, I think again about the other hands that have touched them. Trying to figure out where my beans might have originated, I end up with multiple options. Because they are the Arabica variety, they are most likely from Central or South America. Working and living conditions for the source of my coffee vary by location as well as cultivation techniques. Mountain farms, jungle plantations, small-scale and large-sized commercial operations all participate in the global coffee growing network. Because my bag offers no information about the country of origin, the beans could have been cultivated under widely different conditions.

My initial online search brings up a variety of images of coffee plantations, any of which could have supplied beans for my morning. If they came from Central America, they might have been grown in richly foliated green hillsides where workers are housed in a rustic dormitory during planting and harvesting. In that location, coffee workers wake early. The rising sun finds its way through the slatted walls as the workers begin to stir on hard wooden cots. Because these laborers live near the equator, their days do not change much in length or temperature throughout the year. Even in the morning, the heat is palpable in the crude barn-like structures where the workers sleep. Between forty and sixty people might live in this open warehouse.

A website called *The Daily Coffee* News provides more details in a piece titled "Farmworkers Left Behind: The Human Cost of Coffee Production." The article is ten years old, but I wonder if much has changed.[1] The journalist suggests that in farmworker housing in Central America, families have only a handful of mattresses or blankets among them and no privacy or secure place to keep any personal belongings. Just a few latrines are available, with none in the fields. Most washing is done in the river nearby. As they prepare for work, many workers opt to keep their children with them, aware that the extra small hands help to fulfill their daily quotas.[2] The days are hot, and the forest provides little shade. The coffee seedlings almost seem to be better cared for than the children of the workers, since the tender shoots of the plants are watered and shaded until they are robust enough for planting. The contrast between the value placed on a global commodity and that of the local children is striking. My beans may have come in part from the children's labors.

Though Brazil and Columbia supply four or five times the amount of coffee as Central America, I continue to read about Guatemala, where small farms offer an alternative to the larger plantations. About twelve acres, they are under the cultivation of a single family. About 25 million people grow coffee for a living and their harvests are largely bid for by corporations who push prices downward since they have a monopoly on the markets. The crop is only harvested once a year, and the income generated must support the entire family who also grow food and timber on the same land. If their farms fail, the land is often cleared or used for the other main cash crop—coca—or simply deforested. The sequestered carbon in the forests is released, contributing its gas to the atmosphere as a direct effect of manipulative market strategies in coffee farming.[3] Coffee cultivation is difficult, but its failure is devastating.

Though likely irrelevant, given the variety of my beans, I read about coffee cultivation in India, where plantation owners provide worker housing of tiles and brick, with kitchens and latrines, outdoor water sources, and firewood for cooking. More than fifty-percent of the women workers there are illiterate, but workers are paid for their time, not by piece, and the government mandates accumulation of paid leave, overtime, and regulates labor issues. Still, even in these comparatively better circumstances, the overall economic condition of coffee plantation workers, particularly women, is poor. Intermittent labor and under-employment create permanent insecurity and the work is physically demanding. My leisurely morning coffee is clearly produced at a cost to others. Wealth inequality is a global concern in which "fair trade" practices meant to improve living standards and monitor environmental effects barely have an impact.

I find out that certain characteristics of coffee contribute to the labor issues. Coffee is an "understory" crop, which means it grows well in forested areas and does not require cleared fields. However, that means it is also mainly picked by hand. Nimble fingers and practiced gestures are required to strip the "cherries" from the narrow twig-like branches on which they grow. A keen eye and discerning sense of the condition of ripeness is essential for expert harvesting. In more selective approaches to harvesting, pickers take only the ripe cherries at each pass and return a week or so later to harvest the next group as the beans change color. Mechanical harvesting is possible only where the plants are grown in flatter fields at larger scale, such as areas of Brazil. There the mechanical pickers use diesel-driven hydraulic pumps that spin picking rods whose oscillations cause the coffee beans to fall from the trees and roll into conveyors to a holding bin. A single operator can manage the machine, but all beans are picked at the same time, regardless of maturity. This delays the sorting of mature and green beans to the next stage of the process. The mechanical process is efficient, but a portion of the harvest will be discarded as unacceptable.

In the work of hand gathering, a skilled picker can gather between two and four kilos (approximately four to nine pounds) of cherries an hour. A common daily quota is forty-five to fifty kilos, which means a minimum of ten hours of work. Quick, well-practiced fingers strip the berries from the branches and slip them into a cloth pouch slung across the chest until it is full to bulging. My coffee costs about twelve dollars for a pound and a half of beans, about fifteen minutes' harvest of unprocessed raw beans. Of course, the pickers are not paid in proportion to the retail sale price of the beans which is disconnected from the wages of the farm workers. Most have no contracts, and few rights to assure they are properly compensated. These inequities in global supply chains are of course not unique to the coffee industry. But now I'm curious about what the coffee workers' wages buy in Central America.

To understand the monetary value of the wages of laborers picking this coffee, I consult The Global Living Wage Coalition.[4] They research the real costs of maintaining a "decent" life (secure housing, clean water, access to education, transportation, health care, food and other essentials) anywhere in the world and have been examining the conditions for coffee workers. In certain areas, like Nicaragua, about thirty percent of those picking coffee are under fifteen years of age. In Hawaii, violations of labor laws are rampant, with evidence of children as young as five being forced to pick the cherries. My coffee may have been harvested by a worker in Guatemala where legal minimum wage is under $10 a day or approximately 75 queztals in local currency. In that community one meal at McDonald's costs about 50 queztals.[5] Living Wage reports state clearly that in the rural coffee growing regions of Guatemala workers do not earn enough to support a decent living standard. More than half the country's population lives below the poverty level, and the percentage is much higher in rural areas. The country has the highest level of malnourishment in Latin America, especially outside urban centers. By contrast, Brazil's coffee industry is subject to strict labor legislations that mostly ensure fair labor conditions. But the exceptions include forced and child labor, lack of protective equipment, and poor housing. With an output of nearly 8 billion tons of coffee a year, Brazil is the single largest source of beans. After oil, coffee is among the most lucrative products of "developing" nations. My unsourced coffee beans provide no solid clue about where they have been grown, but in almost no situation does the price I pay translate into a decent wage for laborers.

I continue to delve into the details of the complex industry of coffee farming. Large plantations in the Americas have nurseries where the plants begin as seeds, sprout into seedlings nurtured in the shade, then are transplanted to the soil in the rainy season, a messy and unhealthy task for which workers provide their own boots and ponchos, often improvised from plastic bags. The crop is very vulnerable. A rash of leaf rust can result in massive production losses. For workers this means no employment—no harvest, no work. Insects like cherry borers wreak havoc. The exo-skeletons of their minute bodies have the look of pocked armor, black and shiny, with pith-helmet shaped heads, and they are expert at tunneling into the coffee cherries. Meanwhile another threat comes from the coffee leaf miners, the larval stage of various moths and flies, that burrow through the fresh tender leaves, devastating the plant. In all, nine hundred species of fungi, bacteria, insects and other pests can attack coffee. Against the mounds of dark moist earth, the young plants are a startling green, an attractive food source in the bright sun from which they draw the light essential for photosynthesis, breathing out fresh oxygen. The tender shoots are attractive to many predators.

To protect the plants against attack from some of these pests, a worker applies spray from a can strapped to their back. Sometimes they wear shorts and sandals, go without gloves or respirators. Occasionally they have light protective gear and masks. In Central America, the mountains stretch away in the distance, green-blue with verdant growth, offering scenes of dramatic beauty. But as the pesticides disperse through the forest, they suffuse the air and soil, seeping into the ground and water, washed from the surface of the plants and into the broad environment.

Many, even most, of these pesticides are outlawed in the United States, but still sold to other nations. Their very names have vaguely threatening tone—*disulfoton, thiodan, dursban, parathion, triadimefon*.[6] All are classified from slightly to extremely hazardous based on human risk. But the substances spread through the ecosystem also produce high rates of mortality in birds and mammals. Many of these products are being phased out internationally thanks to an agreement made in Stockholm in 2011, but the high concentrations in water and animals move the toxins up the food chain also passing through skin and contaminated air. The chemicals disturb the function of nerve cell membranes, stimulating uncontrolled excitation in the neurons and disturbing regulatory activity, causing insect nervous systems to collapse. As these chemicals seep into the human systems as well, they cause side effects in individuals and across social groups whose behaviors become erratic.

Information on pesticides is abundant, and readily available. Within a few clicks of my search trail, I find out how the organic damage from pesticides affects neurological and reproductive systems as well as breathing, digestion, and the urinary tract. Tremors and seizures result from exposure. About two million individuals are affected by pesticide poisoning each year. About ten percent of these die. That is 200,000 people. Perversely, it is estimated that only about one percent of the pesticide reaches the targeted pests while much of the rest, spread throughout the environment, is also carried on clothing and skin into the homes of the workers. In a site like the rustic dormitory described earlier, with its limited hygiene facilities, every contact has the potential to transfer toxins from one person to another, including children, through contaminated clothing and other sources.

A report from one community describes a child with malformed hands clawing the air with awkward motions near a young beardless man with the physique of a boy whose sexual maturity has been deferred by several years. Not long ago, members of one community watched as a disoriented, trembling man staggered from the dormitory soiled by diarrhea, then collapsed with convulsions and died. The birds, who breathe the same air, often fall from the sky and trees, their small, vividly-feathered bodies shaking with spasms as they die.

My coffee beans are part of this cycle, my morning habit linked to this geographically distant location, immediately connected to these conditions and consequences. My vague knowledge of coffee cultivation is rapidly becoming explicit and detailed. So far, many different hands have planted beans, watered seedlings, and applied pesticide.

Harvesting and Processing: Picky work
I am just beginning to see the ways my image of coffee as a direct farm to bag product is based on ignorance. The stages the beans will go through before I shake them into the coffee grinder are becoming more apparent, and neither harvesting nor processing are simple. For instance, during the harvest season in Central America, where the work is done by hand, the bags of newly-picked coffee beans are dumped into large baskets throughout the day. The workers' contributions are weighed and recorded. Once the beans are harvested, they are cleaned of twigs and debris on open tables around which the workers stand for hours, sorting through batch after batch. Green unripe

cherries are picked out to be discarded. Then the beans are laid in the sun on wide open trays to dry, or placed directly on asphalt or cement patios in the unobstructed light. The moisture content gets reduced through exposure to open air and sunlight. The hulls gradually shrivel and harden as someone regularly rakes the beans and shifts them from spot to spot. Meanwhile the ground reheats and dries out again. In this "dry" method, the beans remain unwashed and the drying takes from one to two weeks before the hull hardens enough for the dried outer layer to crack off the actual bean. Since they are out in the open, the beans require constant monitoring and must be covered with plastic if it rains. The open patios and drying beds are large and exposed, so in some places mechanical driers are used to speed and better control the process. Heat generated on the concrete and open areas escapes into the air, creating a thermal by-product. This work is hot and spread over time, but requires continuous attention.

As it turns out, different varieties of coffee require different kinds of processing. Wet processing is the main alternative to the dry method just described. Again, since I have no idea of the precise source of my coffee, any of these local practices might have been involved in what creates my morning brew. Arabica beans take less water for processing than some other varieties and what is used can be recycled. In conventional wet processing the beans are put into flotation pans to separate overripe cherries, which are plucked out by hand, from ripe ones. The soaking leaves the beans with a sticky, mucilage layer on them, a process which produces fermentation to aid in shedding the hull. The beans sit in this juice without any additional liquid, slowly fermenting as their covering is digested by bacteria and natural enzymes exuding organic by-products. Sometimes the beans are immersed in tanks of water, where the mucilage begins to ferment, giving off a slightly pungent odor, another contribution to gas in the atmosphere.

These different processes affect the taste of the final drink. Dry fermentation leads to sweeter taste, while the wet beans produce a brighter, drier flavor. In the wet processing, significant amounts of water are required. One estimate was 10,000 cubic meters for each ton of coffee. A single cubic meter is the equivalent of about three bath-tubs of water, which gives some idea of scale. If you took one bath a day, it would take about a hundred years to consume the amount of water used to wash one ton of coffee. From the figures for processing a ton we can come down in scale. It takes about a hundred and forty liters of water to process the half cup of beans used for my morning pot of coffee, or half a bath-tub. Sometimes the wet process molds the beans, and then a musty residue remains with them, affecting their taste and odor, releasing spores into the air that spread opportunistically through breezes and wind currents, aggravating asthma, allergies, and other respiratory ills.

Machine-assisted modes have been developed to aid in removing the sticky layer (de-mucilage) by scrubbing instead of using fermentation and water. This shortcut contributes less pollution, since neither the fermentation residue nor the water used for washing gets consumed in such high volume. This also reduces the impact on local water systems and fisheries. But the pollution in this wastewater can be more than thirty times that of urban sewage. Also, these machines require their own production, energy, and handling in a system of interlinked processes and supply lines whose investigation would lead into another infinite regress of interconnected global systems for producing equipment and consuming fuel and electricity. Every step of these processes involves yet more resources.

Whether processed wet or dry, the outer skin on the bean, known as the *pergamino*, becomes easy to remove, and is sloughed off as the beans rub and tumble. Among coffee afficiandos, one very esoteric bean fermentation, treasured for its outcome, is performed by the picky Civet cat who eats only the best and most ripe coffee cherries, and eliminates them fully fermented. This particular coffee variety, known as Kopi Luwak, is only made in Indonesia where the Civet cats, dark-furred and nocturnal, live in the forests. Their excreted beans are gathered by skilled harvesters paid about $20 a kilogram. The market price for this gourmet rarity is more than thirty times that by the time it reaches customers in a washed and roasted state. The civets (who are related to mongeese) get nothing from this, except, perhaps, the dubious satisfaction of an elite status of which they are likely unaware. They live in the highlands of Sumatra, where the air is thin and the

Part One: Making Coffee   39

Diagram 1: Coffee production

The beans are planted by hand. Pesticides are applied, with consequences. The ripe "cherries" are picked according to their condition, then sorted and unripe beans discarded. They are laid out in the sun where they are raked as they dry. Then the beans are soaked to soften their outer shell, which must be removed by grinding or scrubbing. The dry beans are put into sacks, shipped to destination points for roasting, and then sold to consumers.

heights are wreathed in mist. The beans are harvested and processed quickly—within three hours—so that they are not allowed to denature through exposure. Washed in a mountain spring, dried in a secure environment at a constant temperature and humidity, the precious beans are aged under tight supervision. These are the most precious beans in the world, and they produce very little waste in their processing. Even the water used in washing is preserved, analyzed, and returned to the wild landscape where the civet cats continue their nocturnal digestion, exhaling their own abdominal gases, no doubt, along with the fermented beans. Still, in terms of affluvia, this is a small volume to contribute to global pollution. Now, after this detour to visit the exotic animals, let's go back to the more standard procedures of the "wet" processing method. When the beans have finished their ferment-and-wash cycle, they are dried until hard and then they get sorted by size and color so that defective beans as well as debris are eliminated. If any of the sticky fruit residue—that fermented shell–remains, it also must be removed. In less technologically complex environments, like Yemen, that involves sliding the beans between millstones, a truly ancient technology dating back thousands of years. In more mechanized conditions machine parts whack away at the beans in a gentle rhythm. Again, my beans could have come through any of these processes and I have no way of knowing as a consumer which was the path to my kitchen. On their way through the plantation the harvested beans have now been touched by those who plant, harvest, sort, spread, rake, and scrub them or help them move through various machines.

Sorting: Up in the air
I'm already exhausted by describing the number of steps involved in coffee cultivation. The illusion of beans grown, harvested, roasted, and put into bags has exploded into scenes of physical labor and complex processes involving water, pesticides, waste, and pollution. But we are far from finished. In fact, the beans are still on the coffee plantation.

At this stage, the beans get sorted for size, but I can't

picture the scene, only the processes. The methods run the gamut from least to most technologized. The beans can be blown into the air so that they land in positions corresponding to their weight, with chaff flying away on the breeze—a relatively direct physical approach. Other sorting methods send the mass of beans through a sequence of sieves with graduated holes—a fairly simple mechanical technique except that it involves conveyor belts and custom-made screens in coordinated motion. In another automated process, a vibrating apparatus separates the beans by mass, using the force of gravity to make the lighter beans vibrate in one direction and the heavier in another. But where do they go and what directs their pathways? Metal chutes? Conveyor belts? As if this is not enough, the beans then get sorted by color. In many places this means sorting by eye and by hand—back to basic labor. This is often women's work, and individuals stand for hours picking out beans identified as defective green cherries.[7] Sensor driven mechanisms can simulate this activity and eliminate the "bad" beans by using a puff of compressed air to drive them from the stream of beans rolling by, but these devices are expensive and hard to finance. In addition, they eliminate jobs for the women and younger workers in the rural communities, so are not popular. The supply of these workers is abundant, particularly in remote agricultural areas, so computerized color sorters are mainly concentrated in more developed regions like Brazil and Hawaii, where these highly sophisticated purpose-specific devices are cost-effective. Are they large? Small? In factory rooms? Do the beans roll by or run down planks or chutes? What sound does this make?

After the sorting, the coffee is graded for quality according to size, where it was grown, how it was prepared (wet/dry), and how it tastes. Imperfections lower the grade, so the presence of pebbles or sticks in a batch can be disastrous. But who sets the standards for this grading? Invisible industry networks hover at every turn appearing at crucial moments in the supply chain. On-site and in-depth research would be required to discover these systems.

The beans will need to be roasted, so now they are packed in jute (or burlap) bags which are sewn shut for shipping. Should we track the lifecycle of jute? Or just mention that jute is a very inexpensive crop and grows in India and Bangladesh in abundance. Add a few other facts. High in cellulose and lignin (wood-like elements), jute makes a super-strong fiber that is resistant to heat and water and is easy to dye. The jute plant is adept at absorbing carbon dioxide and gives off lots of oxygen. A single hectare can consume about 15 tons of carbon and create about 11 tons of oxygen within a year. But the jute also must be harvested, processed, spun into string and woven in its own cycle of cultivation in rain-fed, warm, and sunny conditions involving local labor. The bags are fitted with plastic inner linings manufactured from petroleum, another link to extraction industries to which we will return frequently. The bags play a key role in protecting and containing the precious beans until they are delivered safely to their roasters. The bags must not insulate the beans entirely from air–the beans need to breathe–but they must prevent them from getting wet.

These loosely woven, classic, coffee bags are often decorated with vivid, bold printed graphics declaring their origins. This identifying information is applied by silkscreen or stamped with blocks. The pigments and ink binders have their own history, as do the printing techniques and equipment, workers, conditions, and their skills. Screen printing and paint sprayed through stencils, both popular approaches to putting vivid labels on the jute bags, also release chemical vapors from lacquers and aerosols used in the process into the air. Someone designs the labels, draws and cuts the stencils or makes printing blocks. Where are these shops and who works in them?

Tracking every aspect of this one component of the coffee beans' journey and the production of the jute bags would send us on a long detour. Instead, follow the beans as they are shipped and then roasted, getting ever closer to the consumer and my morning routine.

Packing and roasting: Trucks and travels
From wherever they have been collected and packed, the bags of beans are put into crates by human hands, trucked to export depots, and loaded into shipping containers to be distributed around the world. I imagine scenes of forklifts and docks, trucks and drivers, wooden palettes (made where?) and rope (from what?) for securing loads, people (who?) checking inventory and monitoring the process. This leads to the investigation of transportation across these multiple stages. Even with a superficial glance, these processes are embedded in their own histories of production and ongoing sustainability challenges.

For instance, emissions regulations on trucking industries vary considerably around the globe. In many environments, dust and exhaust blend in the air along unpaved stretches of roads from rural plantations before they reach the docks. The precious beans must be kept dry *en route* for however long it takes for them to wend their way to a destination, so the stacked jute bags will be protected by tarpaulins or plastic sheeting made somewhere by someone from some materials. Someone else wraps and ties these in place. More hands.

At the port, the palettes of bagged coffee enter a massive shipping system, going into containers with goods of every kind from multiple sources, all moving in the freight stream of global supply lines. This involves cargo lifts, the decks and holds of vast ships flying under various flags each with a crew and ship that needs to be supplied with food and drink, fuel, waste handling and energy, communications systems, and navigation instruments. Dizzying.

At their destination, the beans are offloaded, taken from the containers. By whom? They are again put onto trucks, and taken to distribution centers that are specialized to serve the coffee industry. Clipboards, computerized tracking systems, inventory supervision are all embedded in their own operations, dependent on other subsidiary industries and infrastructures. At the distribution point, the beans have different fates depending on whether they are going to specialty customers who want to do their own roasting or to companies who roast at the commercial scale. At this stage, the beans, processed and clean, are still in their green condition, useless for brewing. In the case of my beans, a Whole Foods brand, the roasting takes place in Colorado, so they will have gone by rail or truck halfway across the continent whether they came through the port of Long Beach, Houston, Newark or elsewhere.

Reading through various studies of roasting processes, I am immersed in another specialized vocabulary—as in the case with any industry. One site breaks the roasting process down into six steps from "intake" to "packaging."[8] The discussion of "intake solutions" immediately focuses on debris, the necessity of cleaning the beans one more time to remove "unprocessed product"—a euphemism for various kinds of unwanted dirt. Emphasis on efficiency and avoiding contamination from "defective" beans stresses control and consistency for large or micro-lots that are sent to "precision-engineered" steel silos for "de-gassing" and storage. People are hardly mentioned in the description. The grinding phase stresses a "compression-free" process that slices without crushing, offering "superior particle control" that preserves the coffee's "micro-cells." A photograph of a razor-sharp grinding blade shows the edges of its angled teeth glittering. I am struck by the refinement and degree of specialization, by the attention to detail and the use of professional knowledge to promote marketable and commodified expertise in the form of bins, blades, and monitoring devices. Each of these technologies, in turn, has its history and lifecycle in their manufacture, but in order to avoid the rabbit hole of all the specialized machines and technologies involved, I return to the beans.

At last, we get to the roasting. When they arrive at the plant, the heavy bags are manually hoisted from the palettes and hauled up with chains on pulleys by employees for whom this is daily work. The line of cord that has sewn the top closed is pulled, the sack gapes open, and a member of the roasting team digs their hands into the piles of beans. The beans are directly touched again. Light from the plastic lining of the bag glints in contrast to the dull fiber of the jute and the opaque flatness of the beans. Then the beans spill into the large roasting chambers. These are capable of heat up to 400 degrees, and in their spinning drum, the beans will be kept in motion.

Combining roasting times with temperatures is an art, but it is also an environmentally polluting process. The flavor of the coffee depends in part on the bean type and processing, but roasting can make or break the flavor. The beans that go into the drums are green, and can even be soft, still spongy. Afterwards they will be brittle and crunchy with concentrated flavors and delicate oils. A chemical process happens in the heat, and the coffee beans begin to break down at the cellular level. Light roasts leave the oil intact in the bean while darker roasts soak the oil out of the bean to its surface, producing a rich sheen. Carbon dioxide and water vapor are formed causing the cell walls in the beans to crack. Much of the carbon dioxide remains in their porous structure, but outgassing begins somewhere around 356 degrees Farenheit, the temperature for roasting chicken. How is the exhaust channeled and to where? Temperatures for dark roasts are a little more than a hundred degrees higher. While they are roasting, the beans release many of the pesticide toxins they have absorbed into the air. Who is in the room? Who monitors the roasting process? Watches it? Times it? Breathes nearby? Photographs of commercial coffee roasting factories show shiny aluminum machines, clean surfaces, clear air, mechanized environments almost empty of people—except for close-up images of hands dipping into freshly roasted beans.

Literally hundreds of chemical reactions occur in the roasting process. These include formation of a substance known as acrylamide, believed to be a carcinogen at very high levels of concentration—far greater than that in brewed coffee. Volatile organic compounds (VOCs), carbon monoxide, nitrogen oxide and various kinds of particulate matter—this latter most dangerous to those workers in close proximity to the process or the exhaust ducts—are all visible emissions.[9] The fumes released in roasting pose a dangerous health hazard for workers, attacking the lung's airwaves, causing scar tissue to build up, and threatening airflow. Fatal lung disease occurred in a poorly ventilated coffee processing plant in Texas, but the negative effects occur in many stores and shops where roasting occurs and literally takes workers' breath away. Thermal pollution is another by-product that passes invisibly into the atmosphere. The regulation of the coffee roasting industry is not very robust, though awareness of its environmental impact is growing as off-gassing from the roasting process clearly contributes to pollution.

The roaster itself is an elaborate, custom-made machine, a rolling drum tumbler with many geared parts. An electric motor heats filaments above the grill that keeps the beans from coming into direct contact with the heating elements. The beans are fed into a metal funnel. The sound of their small bodies hitting the surface rings like a rain of beads as they flow steadily into the chamber. Belts and pulleys spin the tumbler and keep the beans in constant motion. The chamber is sealed for pressure and the heat begins to mount. A small glass porthole provides a view into the interior. The heat rises. An operator monitors the temperature dial, the heat rises some more, and the color of the beans begins to change as they fly by the porthole. A brass handled instrument on the end of the chamber is designed so that a sample of the beans can be removed without interrupting the spin. The handle is given a twist and pulls out a small trough containing a sample of the beans. For an experienced operator, smell and color are indicators, as well as the degree of shine.

The operator continues the activity, repeating the actions as the heat rises. The beans shift from green to light brown and then darken. An exhaust fan helps regulate the heat and sucks out any chaff that remains on the beans following the earlier stages of processing. The chaff is light and yellowish and flies through the air with ease as the beans remain in motion down below. Chaff is biodegradable and can be composted if a work stream has been established for its disposal. Otherwise, it is simply thrown away. When the beans are deemed finished, the operator opens a brass handled door and drops them onto a perforated surface below where they are gently rotated by a mechanical arm until they cool. After that, the operator opens a trapdoor so the beans can race down a polished metal chute, ready for packaging. This equipment has been manufactured to custom specifications from steel, brass, heating elements, and other materials. At this point, no more jute bags or large containers are in play. The coffee is put into branded packaging for retail consumption. We'll get to that bag in a minute.

The coffee has already been handled by planters, harvesters, rakers, sorters, cleaners, baggers, shippers, and then roasters. In the retail phase, packaging, shelf-stocking, and the work of cashiers, staff, and store managers factors into the final cost, which, as mentioned above, is between ten and twenty dollars a pound. How can this be sustainable if every worker in the supply chain is to be paid a living wage within their own social and economic circumstances? Already the coffee production has introduced pesticides into the lungs, lives, and environments of workers. It has released fermented waste and water into streams and food supplies. It has given off excess heat and toxic fumes from the roasters, consumed energy in the process of packing, shipping, and transportation, and, in some areas, its cultivation contributes to deforestation. This list just focuses on the beans, not the many subsidiary industries essential to their production—equipment manufacture, fuel and energy supplies, labor of trucking and shipping—the list spirals out like an exploding galaxy, a four-dimensional weave of interlocking patterns across space and time.

• •

The Bag: Industrial processes of all kinds
To refill the glass jar, I take a bag of coffee from the freezer. By contrast to the story of the beans, which could be traced through human hands, the tale of the bag leads through massive industries at global scale.

These connect to ancient metal work, 19th century chemists, and surprisingly, the development of hay baling methods.

Start with a description of the bag. The top is pinched by a shining tin-tie of aluminum-foil covered wire, a familiar common object that seems like an afterthought. The bag is coated entirely with a smooth layer of orange ink, so perfectly applied it feels bonded to the substrate. Against this background, in bright green lettering, "Fair Trade" is blazoned prominently, reassuring me my consumer choices are conscientious. Designs in brown and green fill up the front, sides, and back of the bag, including an identifying logo for the brand, information about the integrity of the source, the blend of beans, and other readily ignored information. The design shows an icon of a bright sun, a bee, and a few green leaves suggesting a happy harmonious natural cycle of productive growth. A small statement guarantees these are non-GMO, organic. The package reinforces my misperception that the beans are a simple farm-to-table product whose arrival into my kitchen involved little more than putting them into a bag. The labor of farming, harvesting, drying, shipping, and roasting disappears from the experience of opening the bag and pouring out the beans as if they have just arrived from the land, from a smiling worker who cheerfully picked them in the warm bright sunshine.

The coffee smells fresh as the odor of the beans fills the air.

I look again at the package, still struck by the smoothness of the surface. The pale, matte peachy ink slides under the touch, its satin surface utterly frictionless. Along with the assurances that the coffee is not genetically modified, the green leaves in the logo communicate a happy message of eco-friendly production. The organically-themed package is meant to slip into my hands without causing irritation or disturbance, its soothing design providing reassurance—this is carefree consumption. But what regulatory agencies are indexed by these tiny statements? Again, I wonder who checks for the genetic modifications, supervises the raising, harvesting, and marketing of these beans? Where are the checks and balances against human rights abuses actually implemented so that the label can claim this is a "Fair Trade" product? In the United States, the Fair Trade Federation works to insure good working conditions and environmental sustainability.[10] But, still, how is the profit margin on my bag of beans calculated given all of the people and processes involved in getting the coffee to this point?

I buy my beans from Whole Foods, this means Amazon, the largest distribution network in America, possibly the world, and its abuses are rampantly evident in daily life—the trucks, the cardboard, the shipping, the warehouse workers, the large and small scale impacts, other labor issues. I am reeling. Just reaching for my beans puts me at the consumer endpoint of a system so enormous it staggers my mind as I begin to grasp its multiple aspects. Am

I guilty of ecological crimes simply by being oblivious to the elaborate chains of connection on which I depend? I wonder whether it is ethical to consume coffee or any other product I do not grow myself? But even then... nothing is outside of the cycles of production and their elaborate co-dependencies. Growing my own food would just put me into different supply chains and systems.

I am just beginning to analyze the second item in my ten-minute coffee-and-cat-food morning routine. By the time I am finished, my mind will be overwhelmed. Going from the beans to the bag shifts our story radically from one of human hands to one rooted in the petrochemical industries.

PET, the plastic film: A massive industry
I know very little about packaging, or the costs and impacts of its manufacture. The bag I am looking at is a mystery. I begin with basic queries to find out how many types and categories of bags are used for coffee beans. The one in which my beans are packaged is what is known as a "high barrier" type, and it is ideal for coffee and tea storage because of the shiny, flexible plastic foil laminate of which it is made.

Pause for a moment and think about that phrase, "flexible plastic foil laminate," and all that it suggests. Various discrete materials are layered to create an inexpensive, lightweight, disposable but durable sack. The plastic and foil materials get their characteristic flexibility as the result of complex manufacturing techniques. While I might be able to pick and sort coffee beans if I had to, if I were to try to make plastic out of petroleum, I would fail at every point from the very beginning.

Some coffee bags are made of aluminum foil or paper, but my "flexible plastic" is created with PET, polyethylene terephthalate, a chemical substance whose composition I start to research, along with its lifecycle and manufacture. My high school chemistry does not get me very far here. I cannot even parse the components in its name beyond the prefix "poly" which suggests something in multiples. This turns out to be the number of strands in the chemical structure, but that doesn't get me very far in terms of understanding how this material comes into being.

My trail of clicks through internet sites seeking information on PET reveals lovely images of carbon, hydrogen, and oxygen atoms bonded in a regular pattern in what seems to be a potentially infinitely repeatable string. Nice. The diagrams are highly aesthetic, but still leave me unenlightened about the compound and its production.

It turns out that PET was invented in the 1940s and produced industrially beginning in the 1950s as part of a major boom in creating synthetic materials. Earlier plastics like celluloid (from cellulose, a common vegetable fiber) and viscose (from wood pulp) were 19th century inventions. They used organic materials directly as their base—dissolving wood fiber in alcohol and mixing some oil or wax into the pulp. While chemistry is involved, the process can be imagined as a physical one. I feel like I could cook cellulose in a shed if I wanted. But in the 20th century, "true" plastics began to appear, that is, materials synthesized chemically at an industrial scale. With generic names like vinyl, nylon, and acrylic, they have long been part of common vocabulary, their origins obscured by their familiarity. Among these chemically produced synthetics, PET is part of a group referred to as "thermoplastics"—indicating that heat is an important part of their production process.

All this time, I am holding the coffee bean bag in my hand wondering where this trail will lead in terms of pollution and ecological cost.

I start with the technical name of PET, polyethylene terephthalate. I discover that both of its components, (poly)ethylene glycol and terephthalic acid, are organic compounds, which simply means they contain carbon atoms that are bonded to other atoms—mainly hydrogen and oxygen. As with all compounds, the structure is everything—where bonds form and how the atoms are configured is what determines the properties of the material.

Carbon is the basic element of life, living things would

not exist without it, and it is found in all fossil fuels—coal, petroleum, and natural gas. The plastic in my coffee bag is made of once-living organisms, the ancient forests and animals of prehistoric times. An industry site describes the steps in the production process from "raw materials" through "esterification," "polycondensation," "solid-state polymerization," "extrusion and pelletization," to "manufacturing products."[11] Most of these terms are not familiar enough for me to conjure an image of what they mean, but I gather that by processing petroleum using heat, water, pressure, and chemical reactions, a mass of generic plastic material is produced as a flexible solid in pellet form that can be shaped into bottles, packages, or pliable sheets. At each stage of the process, heat waste, by-products, and above all, energy consumption make the ecological production costs high. When I search for images of a PET manufacturing plant, I find huge installations with enormous silos, conveyor belts, vats, pressure cookers, and industrial equipment constantly fed by a stream of raw materials, mainly coal and petroleum—and constantly producing waste.

A more detailed description of the production of PET includes terms like "column-type reactor" used for "esterification" and in the process "methanol recovery" and "purification" essential to prevent significant levels of VOC (volatile organic compound) emissions (on which more ahead). These technical terms for these complex processes refer to activities ongoing every day and on which

the daily use of many products depends. But the details for each individual part of the process are complex. For instance, the "methanol recovery" system in the factory has its own elaborately engineered design to distill the gas into vapor, condensates, and other products that each have to be processed in turn to neutralize their effect on the atmosphere or allow them to be recycled and reused. In other words, every step of the manufacturing process

Part One: Making Coffee   59

Diagram 2: PET Plastic production

Remains of dinosaurs, other organisms, and ancient forests which now exist as petroleum and oil reserves. Fracking methods and/or pumping puts the oil and gas into pipelines to a chemical processing plant. The fumes and particulate matter released into the air cause damage to lungs and add to carbon emissions. Large industrial plants process the chemicals into a mixture that is then turned into a dry powder. Waste water carries toxins into the environment. The non-stop pipelines create massive amounts of ingredients for plastic which are then mixed, heated, and output as pellets and sheets. Used plastic creates huge waste sites and also gets into landfill and ocean habitats where it is a hazard to marine life.

is its own specialized industry. If I were to describe the production of PET in full detail, my book would explode.

The crucial point for my coffee bag is that the processes result in a highly versatile plastic commonly used to make fibers and textiles. PET is the material used to create clear plastic packaging like the clamshell boxes used for salad greens and other perishables. Its flexible properties allow it to spring back into shape if it is pinched or squashed, and the film does not retain creases the way aluminum or paper would, as every supermarket shopper knows from handling the many containers in which food products are packaged. It is also one of the most efficient plastics to recycle. Essentially, it can be collected, cleaned, shredded, melted and made into pellets or sheets again. That description of recycling makes it sound smooth and unproblematic, which is what the industry wants us to believe. But even the manufacturers admit their industry is energy intensive, though progress is being made on sustainability, such as switching to plant-based renewables as the raw materials. Instead of relying solely on by-products of petroleum and shale gas, the new processes could use bio-based sources. Precisely what these are, how they also must be treated, and what the ecological costs of their production might be remains unclear. Industry websites use the term "bio-based feedstocks" generically without providing any detail.

The PET in my coffee bag was produced as sheets.

It is the ideal material for creating the moisture and light proof linings for the sacks in which coffee beans are sold. PET is strong, but it is also "inert"—which means that it shouldn't react, even with a substance as chemically complex as coffee beans.

The sheer scale of the presence of PET-based objects in our daily lives is mind-boggling. For instance, the making of plastic consumes almost all the world's supply of (TPA) terephthalic acid, one of the two compounds that make PET. As already mentioned, TPA can be derived from organic materials, like turpentine, but it is generally manufactured in a lab and then stored in giant silos in powdered form. The raw materials are petrochemicals—oil derivatives–but getting to the start point of the supply chain proves difficult. Finding out, for instance, that PET is made by "polymerization" (turning compounds into long strands) of ethylene glycol and terephthalic acid still leaves me stranded. What is the source of those substances? The first is derived from ethylene. Ok, and where is that found? The second is made from xylene. Same question. The latter is a coal-tar distillate, it seems—which means what in terms of production? And the first is also derived from natural gas and petroleum.

The best I can do in terms of understanding the way ethylene is processed is a diagram that shows a tank of gas fed through a stirring device and sending out some kind of slurry that is in turn washed, filtered, and dried while spinning off various by-products and waste along the way. Apparently, in Hurricane Harvey in 2017, the supply chain for this essential material broke down. The petrochemical refineries in the Houston Ship Channel, giant plants where natural gas is heated to crack its molecular bonds, had their operations disrupted by the storm. Is the southern United States the location where about three-quarters of the world's ethylene is produced? Any photograph of the petrochemical industries features the same elements—men in hard hats, carrying clipboards, standing on metal scaffolding structures with tanks, pipes, and valves in view. For the moment, this is my limit for tracking the raw materials of ethylene and xylene from petroleum to product. Now, let's address the TPA (terephthalic acid).

This large-scale industry produces about 2 million tons of TPA a year.[12] (The weight of the Great Pyramid of Egypt is estimated at about 5.7 million tons, so imagine a new pyramid of TPA appearing and disappearing every three years. The powder is mixed with the liquid, ethylene glycol (whose production we traced schematically above), into a flexible viscous paste. Conjure an image of white glue and you will be close to the texture. The mixing takes place in a custom-manufactured tank that is designed to spray the glycol through multiple slots so that it can be blended with the ethylene by mixer-paddles that knead it constantly in different directions. This paste is then sent through another set of processes of heating and pressure that creates by-products all along the way before it is dried. In this way, the powder for TPA gets created. Still feels like a long way from my coffee bag.

More research produces more questions. For instance, one stage of TPA production includes an "oxidation" process using equipment that is coated with titanium in which a corrosive catalyst can act. Ok, I basically grasp this, but coated with titanium? Isn't that expensive? I try reading about titanium extraction and find that it involves a "pyrometallurgical" process designed to get metals from ore by smelting, roasting, or related techniques. What do any of these industrial processes look like? Once again, we are in the realm of large vats, spinning chambers, vents, pressure valves, and tubes that feed one liquid into another, draw off gas, and have the general appearance of elaborate pressure cookers. All of this just to get the material that lines a tank in one step of a complex process that leads to the plastic in my coffee bag.

If you read through the industry's public relations posts, you find that innovations are happening all the time. One up-to-date plant was designed to produce over 800 million pounds of crude terephthalic acid (TPA) in one year for a value of over 100 million dollars. The designers estimated the single plant, located in the Gulf Coast, would have more than a 34% rate return on investment. This is because TPA plays such a huge role in all aspects of what is succinctly referred to as the contemporary chemical industry.[13] The scale of production of these basic polymer products is enormous, though the industry claims that less than 20% of global petroleum consumption goes into their production. Somehow the idea that a fifth of the world's petroleum goes into plastic does not make the amount seem insignificant. Quite the contrary. In some countries, where the coal industry is less regulated, ethylene glycol, the main raw material for PET, is made from carbon monoxide, though how the gas becomes a pliable plastic is a topic that would require exploring another forking path through fields and disciplines I lack the expertise to follow.

What is clear is that the large chemical industry producers, like Dow and Union Carbide, are searching for "greener" alternatives to the current petroleum-based production by testing methods of creating ethylene from carbon dioxide. Again, the processes involve many specialized methods where high amounts of energy are needed and considerable waste is given off. Whatever innovations occur, the substance, ethylene glycol (an odorless, colorless, sticky and slightly sweet substance), which, by the way, was first made artificially in a lab by a French chemist, Charles-Adolphe Wurtz, in the middle of the 19th century, has turned out to be the universal stuff from which plastics of all kinds are created. Many of Wurtz's innovations in chemistry led to modern products and processes.

Part One: Making Coffee   65

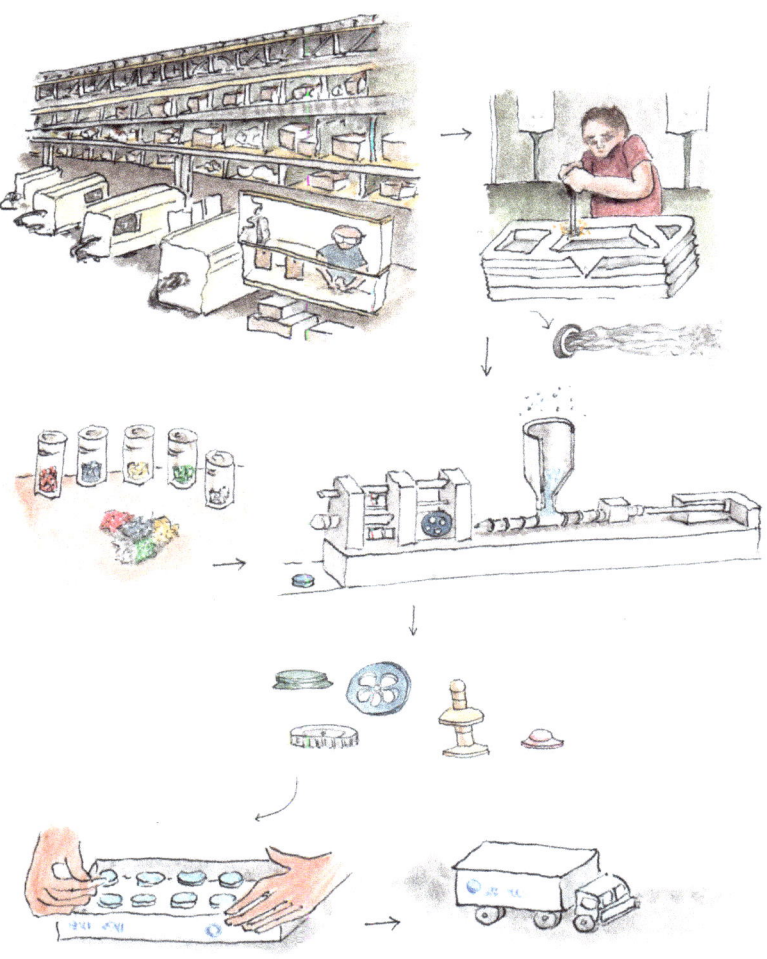

Diagram 3: Gas release valve

A factory for machine work produces metal molds custom designed for specific purposes. Plastic material in the form of pellets, colored by various pigments, will be blown into the molds and released in an ongoing assembly-line of products. These are packed and shipped to be used in assembling the coffee bean bags.

Before we finish with PET, however, let's pause for a moment at the molecular level where the polymer has the appearance of a twisted strand of beads, its specific combination of carbon, hydrogen, and oxygen giving it those properties of flexibility and strength. Of course, the structure is not visible to the naked eye, but the same properties that make it ideal to be made into the shiny bright mylar balloons that are filled with helium for cheerful celebrations make it suitable for the inside coating on film used in packaging coffee. In both cases, that shiny surface is the result of a process of metallization by which aluminum is evaporated onto the plastic film. Yes, metal is evaporated in a thin layer onto the plastic so that these films can become products that range from food packaging to those birthday balloons, space blankets, and rolls of pressure-sensitive tape. The thin PET film comes out of the spinning rollers of a machine shimmering, light, flexible, and void of imperfections. Not a ding or a bruise disturbs the smooth metallic sheen. The plastic is perfect, unmarred, and impermeable. We have witnessed the 21st century equivalent of alchemy. Now PET is in groundwater, drinking water, and other systems essential for survival, one of the forever pollutants, chemicals that persist indefinitely.

All of this chemistry and industrial processing is needed to make the coffee bag with its smoothly coated surfaces. The layers are so tightly bonded they are almost indistinguishable. Between the shiny interior and the outer film of ink, the PET sheet is what has rolled off these huge industrial presses. My bag is made from this metalized film, cut and folded and crimped and then covered with ink. A line of glue holds the pouch closed and serves to attach the thick tin-tie to its top. This tin-tie cracks off immediately as I pull the edges of the pouch apart and hear the quick whoosh of air sucked in as the vacuum seal breaks.

The gas release valve: Taking shape(s)
The design of my coffee sack is known as a gusset pouch, sealed on all seams and finished at the bottom with a pleated fold. The last time I thought about a gusset was in high school when I tried to sew a triangular insert into the underarm of a garment to make it expandable. I failed. Zip locks, hang holes, and tear notches are other common features designed into the pouches for ease of reclosing, display, and opening. Still, each of these small features had to be designed and implemented. Even tear notches require a die-cut stamping process if they are to be added.

But it is the small plastic gas release valve also built into the bag that is my focus here. I've never noticed it before. Almost invisible, its purpose is to assure that any gas produced by the beans can escape without air coming in. About the size of a button, the small valve is inserted into the material of the bag. It is a belly-button that breathes. Two tiny slits cut into the outside of the sack, like the fang-marks of a snake, are the only sign that the valve is present. On the inside, the plastic device is evident, its tiny puck-like form clearly punched into the plastic film.

Turns out that this insignificant feature of the sack, almost undetected, is related to a wide family of release valves in plastic and metal, manufactured in nearly infinite numbers of customized forms for various purposes. One manufacturing site boasted of more than six million varieties, each produced in accord with detailed specifications for the height, width, threads, locking devices, motion of a "poppet" (for monitoring release of vapor) in the shaft of more complex designs with many features.[14] The home page of a site called SmartProducts displayed line after line of these cunning valves. They look for all the world like an assembly of plastic chess pieces gone rogue in their designs. How are they made? One common method is for them to be "blow molded" by taking a molten tube of plastic, putting it into a mold, and inflating the plastic with air until it takes the shape of the cavity. Alternatively, the plastic is injected as a hot soft liquid and takes the shape dictated by the mold without the benefit of inflation. Someone must make the molds and pick the plastic colors, whose production involves dyes and pigments of various kinds. The sources for these connects to a host of other supply lines. Reading about one single example of a chemical used to produce the color blue, cobalt, is devastating. My valve is white, so what substance is it and where did it come from? Every step of analysis raises more questions.

Every metal mold for casting is machined separately. Every shape is purpose-specific. The skill and equipment required to execute this process of production are part of an industry that is constantly pumping out parts and fittings so that precisely made metal molds that have been drilled, threaded, polished and matched can release their output of plastic forms in a steady stream. This tiny bud of a valve arrives in the bag in my freezer through its own global itinerary, and yet, is barely noticeable, just part of the incidental material to be thrown away when the sack is empty. Its production also connects directly to the lifecycle of plastics already described–from petroleum to pellets of versatile material.

Manufacturing begets manufacturing in a filiated lineage of relations. As we have seen, each stage of these industrial processes depends on the expert and specific knowledge of an earlier step–and behind that, one earlier yet. The little button of a valve is the outcome of a plastic molding process that itself depends on die-making with its own vocabulary of manufacture (blanking, piercing, cutting, deforming sheet metal) and assembly (shoes, mounts, pins, plates, guides, shanks, pilots and so on). This lifecycle depends on the profession of machining, precision engineering, and before that of the manufacture of sheet metal, of which the most common type is steel, though aluminum and brass are also used to make machine parts. Steel is an alloy of iron and carbon, also processed under specific and skilled conditions from materials mined and processed in their own long narrative of extraction and refinement. All this for the little button of a valve that I hardly noticed in the bag.

Sticky layers: Ink and adhesive
In addition to the layers of laminated film that compose the sack, detectable only at the very edges where it ends a millimeter or so short of the plastic, a thin skin of printed ink is also bonded to the surface. By now, I have realized that there are about five layers in this sack material: a surface film, printing ink layer, adhesive, the now-familiar plastic film (PET), another adhesive, and an inert, barrier film (LDPE or low-density polyethylene) on the inside near the food product. Moisture-proof and resistant to impact and chemicals, the LDPE layer is the one in contact with the beans and is the truly "inert" barrier.

These plastic layers were all invisible to me until I began to research the complex details of the manufacture of the bag. Each of the thin, flexible five layers, ink and adhesives, as well as the plastics, has its own lifecycle. The phrase "heat-activated thermoplastic adhesives," for

Part One: Making Coffee 71

instance, points to a sub-industry creating materials used to bond one layer with another in the shiny plastic that is used for the coffee bag. Something must get the layers to stick together. And the variety and specificity of these heat-activated adhesives is essentially limitless—like the plastic valves, they can be customized for any process or purpose. Melt-points for these adhesives—the temperature they need to be at for application—hovers between 160 and 280 degrees Fahrenheit, a span below and above boiling point for water, but much above the standard comfort level for a daily shower, which is in the range of 105 degrees. Adhesive production is another specialized process. Another industry.

After they are created and before they are used, the sheets of these thermo-activated adhesives are dry, not tacky. They feel like paper to the touch and it is only when they are heated—thermo-activated—that they begin the chemical process of bonding. Like so many industrially produced substances, the adhesives are polymers—strands of chemical compounds suspended in a condition that keeps them separate from each other until activated. In the common variety of white glue used in kindergartens and craft fairs, the polymer strands become bonded when the liquid evaporates and they can close ranks, hooking their complex structures together permanently. In heat sensitive processes, the polymers get their chance to bond with each other when the extra thermal energy frees them from their static state on the dry sheets to interact with each other. They form bonds quickly, in a moment of polymer speed-dating, and the quick cooling fixes them in a permanent relationship with each other and the substances they are linking.

The chemical industry describes these relationships as cross-linked networks. A reactive polymer (that would be the edgy partner in the couple) and a curing agent (caretaker) meet in a chemical reaction and the change takes place in the rapid cycle of heating and cooling characteristic of many relationship dynamics. The compounds have the suggestive name of "hot melts," and in their processing, no small molecules are eliminated as these polymers form chains by sharing their electrons. All this sounds rather suggestive. The language has a vivid poetry to it and a metaphoric correlation with human behaviors is readily imagined. However, in my coffee bag, all of this simply results in layers so tightly laminated they seem like one sheet of plastic.

Printing: Color for the consumer
We are almost finished with the bag, except for the printed surface and tin tie. The smooth, satiny top surface of the bag is a layer of matte inks in an orange, black-brown, and green in a coffee-related palette. The colors result from the presence of pigments in a binder or substrate. The liquid medium of the ink holds these minute crystalline bits of material suspended. Unlike dyes, which bond with and are transformed by their relation with other materials—the way yarn and cloth fibers are penetrated by stains—pigments

remain intact at the chemical level. The crystals keep their identity and don't change as they are mixed into the ink. Because they are not affected by the substrate, they refract light according to their physical structure and this gives rise to human color perception. The surface of the coffee bag is a scene of silent but vivid optical activity, as light rays bend and refract through the multiple microscopic forms of crystals in the ink. The complexity and magic of this activity can only be seen in the results. The crystals shimmer according to their individual capacity to engage with the optics of light across the electromagnetic spectrum, offering the human eye a palette of colors.

Pigment sources are as varied as the materials of raw earth and the full arsenal of the chemical laboratory. The red ochres and carbon blacks of prehistoric art are still present in our palette. Tens of thousands of years of human history link their use with the activities of artists in the past who prepared their pots of earth by mixing in the charred remains of the fire pit, adding pine resin and other binders with water or spit, and creating a smooth liquid with which to daub the surface of the walls. The pigments connect us to the art of our ancient ancestors, even if the scale of industrial manufacture tips away from the handmade process and into the world of huge furnaces and vats, spinning mechanisms and drying racks. The lineage of both organic and inorganic pigments persists, and could be tracked as surely as other signs of migration, trade, and exchange among ancient humans. Color use and distribution tells its own version of human history. Both natural sources and mineral precursors are extended by the modern distillation of an ever-finer and wider range of colors created in the laboratory.

To be printed, the PET film is sent through the shining rollers of a huge web press. The ink moves from a smooth trough of liquid to become a dry surface in a matter of seconds. What evaporates in the process? Some invisible liquid vaporizes in the process at a speed that is almost inconceivable. The ink dries almost instantly. The sheets pass from the roller through the air and dry as they are wrapped onto the growing roll of finished material. The continuous ribbon of film curls on the core without a hitch as the off-gassing rises. In fact, almost all the pollution created by the printing industry is released into the air, much of it related to the solvents used to keep the ink fluid and help it dry. Discussions of these pollutants describe the "adverse effects" they can have on the human nervous system causing mild symptoms like headache, nausea, and dizziness. Prolonged exposure can cause liver and kidney damage.

The tin-tie: A surprise link to hay bales
The bag is clearly so complicated that I have subdivided its description into more and more topics. The final piece is the bright shiny tin-tie. An "aluminum" paper

Part One: Making Coffee

film is wrapped, glued, and crimped around a flexible wire, the outcome of another series of manufacturing events. That wire, thin and easy to bend, is of a fine gauge. It also had to be produced. Such small wires are made by pulling a metal rod through what is known as a draw plate. In this process the rod is forced through a funneling chamber that reduces its diameter. In the industry, this is known as passing from an "undrawn" to a "drawn" condition. In ancient times, this process was performed using perforated beads, and all the ornamental and functional wires woven into chains in the metalwork of antiquity had to be achieved through this process. The marks on wires from ancient Egypt, some dating back to the 2nd millennium BCE, show evidence they were drawn in this way. From providing settings for the gems and adornments of Pharaohs to the humble task of pinching my coffee bag closed, the drawn wire has descended from its once noble role in the jeweler's art to mere utility.

The twist tie had a specific moment of invention, a birthdate, and a known inventor. In 1961 Charles Burford covered some fine gauge stainless steel wire with a broad paper strip, making it easy to twist and handle. His father had invented an automatic hay baler, and no doubt young Charles had been inspired by the results since he made the technique applicable to baling garbage, among other things. Before he got around to the twist tie, he implemented a device that automatically sprinkled poppy and sesame seeds on hamburger buns in the baking process. For this and other achievements, he was recognized by the American Society Baking Hall of Fame, a group inclined, it seems, to overlook his less savory penchant for bringing back hunting trophies from his African travels (though to his credit, he was also dedicated to saving the black rhino and other endangered animals). Every time you untwist a tie, it connects you to this Oklahoma-born inventor, his father, and their practical farming roots.

The tin-tie was applied at the bag factory with a machine made expressly for this purpose, laying a thin line of adhesive onto the surface so that it holds just long enough to crack off at first use. And as that adhesive dried, what was released into the air? Most pressure sensitive adhesives are made from natural or synthetic rubber resins. They are manufactured using a hot-melt (mentioned above) or solvent based method. The latter requires evaporation so that the adhesive material dissolved in water can be left behind as a usable residue, while hot-melt flows the liquid mixture after heating so it can be easily applied to a substrate. Hot-melt methods produce fewer toxins than solvent based ones, but since these are all thermoplastic polymers whose main raw material is petroleum, the differences are less significant than what the components have in common. The adhesive of the apparently innocuous twist tie is yet another product of a global fossil fuel industry where off-gassing of methane and pollutants from VOCs (volatile organic compounds) are major contributors to ground-level ozone. The petroleum industry releases a whole host of toxins in the benzene family that are known carcinogens. The tiny detail of attaching the tin tie to the coffee bean bag is part of a chain of industrial processes for customized production of adhesives designed so I, the consumer, can snap the silver band free or press it closed to keep my beans fresh.

The beans, their cultivation and journey to distribution, the bag, the inks, the adhesives, and all the systems of labor and equipment along the way are just barely described here, summarily sketched. Many scenes of labor, of waste, of mining, of shipping and hauling, of the intricate interweaving of multiple and many systems at local and global scales are missing (e.g. processing and manufacture of ink pigments). To track any one of these thoroughly leads to a complex of connections that ultimately returns us to the earth as the source for extraction and elaborate industrial scale processing plants and laboratories all producing gaseous, liquid, and solid waste. But now I have at least some sense of what it means to take the coffee bag out of the refrigerator in a habitual—and frankly unconscious—gesture.

• •

Coffee grinder: Magnetism, motor and real steel
With a smooth sliding motion, I push the power button that completes the electrical circuit on my coffee grinder. That simple gesture launches the action of the steel blade. It hums and spins, pulverizing the coffee beans in the chamber. The sharp cracking sound quickly subsides into fine-grained whirring. I release the button and it springs up, breaking

the electrical circuit. The activity seems far from any primal activities such as processing ore or doing metalwork. The mythic image of Vulcan's forge is not in my mind as I sense the beans becoming a fragrant powder. Nor do I smell fumes of naphthalene or nitrogen oxide or see a streaming volume of polluted water where a stinking slag heap slips insidiously into place near a monstrous steel plant whose workings are the endpoint of centuries of human expertise. Yet, all of this is essential to the production of the very ordinary blade in my grinder, an object that would have been almost impossible to mass-produce just a few hundred years ago.

The leveraging of one advance in technology upon another in the history of industrial processes is invisible in these familiar objects. Though I know this intuitively, I am seeing that my everyday actions are embedded in complex dependencies of material life, each with their own elaborate networks connected to cultural relations and collective expertise. I could not build a coffee grinder from scratch. I could not even assemble one from components. I am a consumer making use of an ordinary device that is nonetheless an opaque mystery to me. In his popular video, "Making a Toaster from Scratch," Thomas Thwaites created a dramatic demonstration of the ways industrial processes far exceed the capacity of individuals to produce common objects.[15] The video exposes some of the specifics of manufacturing, peeling back the curtain that hides these from view. What Thwaites's work does not depict are the working conditions, skills, labor, and pollution involved in the actual production of such an object, only the impossibility of replicating their results by hand.

I shake the grounds from the chamber where the blade has completed its work. To use the appliance, I don't need to know anything about the vast systems in which my simple task of grinding coffee is located. I don't need to know about its inner workings. For the most part, I realize again, I live in profound ignorance of the processes on which my daily life depends.

My small electric coffee grinder lives inconspicuously on my counter. Bought decades ago, the mini-appliance has travelled with me from New Haven to Charlottesville and then to Los Angeles. It has even been on vacation to the Outer Banks to provide the pleasure of fresh ground beans at the beach. A loyal object with a proven record of reliable service, its crimes against the environment seem minor, particularly depreciated across its many years in my possession.

Tight, compact, with its hard, outer casing, brown-tinged transparent plastic cap, and shiny interior, the machine appears simple enough: a blade, motor, outer shell, grinding chamber and electrical cord.

But as it turns out, this small appliance has a complex anatomy. A chart known in the industry as a DFMA, "Design for Manufacturing and Assembly," reveals that a comparable new grinder has more than fifty-five components to it. While my older model does not have all the parts needed for up-to-date programmable and variable speed features, it is still remarkably complex. Every tiny element–from the coiled spring that returns the power button to its position or the injection molded plastic slide that completes the circuit–is the outcome of another interconnected manufacturing system. Each of these parts has been stamped, bent, die-cut, or produced by other industrial methods themselves linked to processes of extraction and transformation that leave behind their own trail of pollution and waste. They all generate affluvia.

Digging into the DFMA I find that the *blade sub-assembly*, as the parts chart informs me it is called, is connected to a *blade hub* which is in turn attached to the *drive shaft*. The design document offers other details about the manufacturing of each part. The hub and shaft are created by plastic injection molding (already described in the discussion of the gasket valve), and incorporate a rubber blade washer and gasket to reduce friction and vibration, keeping the mechanism from shaking itself apart. Some suggestively named parts—the female drive adapter, rubber nipples (for vibration isolation and noise reduction, functions far from their anatomical inspiration) and a male drive adapter (yes)–extend this nuclear family of elements. Steel, plastic, copper, rubber and smaller amounts of tin and aluminum, are all present

82 AFFLUVIA

to varying degrees and have been stamped, molded, bent and otherwise shaped. Each part has its history and design for manufacturing and assembly.

My grinder lacks a circuit board, programmable interface, lights, and other features of the up-to-date smart models. It does not play music, communicate with other appliances, or receive text messages. Nor has it advocated for the right to self-determination. But it is still the outcome of a remarkable array of industrial processes.

The spring: Iron ore from the stars
Now consider the tiny coiled spring that returns the circuit-completing button to its resting position. A truly inconspicuous element of my grinder, but one that serves an important purpose by its characteristic flexibility. This thin and delicate wire is made of steel. Steel. Only in use for about the last three and a half millennia, steel is a technology younger than writing or

Diagram 4 (left): Steel production
Ore with iron content is mined in large open pits. So is coal, which can also be mined underground. Damage from running heavy equipment includes hearing loss and motion disorders. Coal is heated in large ovens and transformed into coke. Risks to workers include falls and injuries from equipment and exposure to heat and fumes. The steel plant includes blast furnaces to reduce the amount of carbon in the iron changing is chemical structure. Liquid steel runs from the furnaces to be turned into sheets and rods that can be cast and die-cut into shapes, including blades for the coffee grinder.

accounting. The lifecycle that brings it to my kitchen connects to yet more elaborate industrial technologies and basic scenes of extraction. I interact daily with this invisible part of the machine when I press down with my palm to overcome its slight resistance.

Steel, like plastic, cement, and glass is a common substance, manufactured in great quantities and then specialized for a multitude of tasks. Iron ore, limestone, and coke are the main raw materials, along with scrap steel. This little spring of shiny thin wire provides a connection between my grinder and the industries that scrape the surface of the earth into gaping craters to remove raw ore that itself originated in the cosmos.

Steel production relies on coal and iron. Coal is a primal fossil substance, raw material, able to be taken directly from the earth. But iron extraction is more complex. Both are part of the industries that humans excel at—extraction and transformation. We remove the stuff of millions, billions, of years of life and death, geological processes of volcanism, sedimentation, and compression, and turn it into something else. Other living creatures use the matter of vegetable and animal life, water and air, and process it through their cells, lungs, and guts. But we as a species take the materials of earth and send them through elaborate procedures that reduce their original form to essential compounds with which to mold the machines and devices of our world. In the case of iron, we are extracting an element that can only be made with the heat and energy of a supernova explosion or what the astronomers refer to as a "catastrophic star death." In other words, the iron on earth was created long ago and/or far away somewhere in the universe and then arrived on earth as cosmic dust when the planet was formed or in meteorites crashing to our surface.

Iron ore is abundant, but the process of extracting it from the mixtures in which it is embedded are still energy intensive. The steel industry represents itself as environmentally sound in part because steel is so readily recycled. But the pollutants generated in production are staggering in number and scale.

But let's go back to the scenes of extraction. Iron mining makes open gashes in the earth. Envision a massive crater. The deep-cut sides are stepped with terraces that stretch hundreds of meters in depth, the equivalent of a hundred-story building. In the United States, such dramatic sites are dug out of the landscape of Minnesota, Michigan, Utah among other places, but the chief sources of iron ore for the global markets are in Western Australia where more than five hundred and fifty million tons of ore are extracted yearly. Everywhere these operations take place, the rough-edged cuts appear as deep rich red-brown above the flaming orange of the pit's bottom. The colors seem as fantastic as the surface of Mars and from the rim of the mine down to where water pools in the open gouges of the earth as little evidence of life shows as on that remote planet. Yet the signs of human activity appear in the clear pattern of extraction, the large-scale consumption of a massive volume of raw material. The gaping red raw pit in the earth is a vivid wound from which particulate matter escapes in fine dust to spread on the wind. Multiple health hazards are associated with mining operations. In addition to the obvious threat to lungs from dust, other risks involve traumatic injury, ergonomic issues, and noise, constant and unrelenting noise. All of this is just the beginning of the process by which my steel coffee grinder spring and blade get made.

But for all the redness of that scene, the iron ore turns dark once processed. Iron ore is not a single pure substance, not a concentrated deposit of the basic chemical element, identified by the letters *Fe*, but instead is part of compounds—literally hundreds of them with iron minerals in them. They have vivid names like magnetite, hematite, and siderite and each has a different chemical structure, color, and geological history of its formation. All must be subjected to processes like crushing, grinding, and other physical activities to pull out the iron. Processes known as "magnetic separation" as well as "flotation" and "re-election" suggest the application of procedures that separate the ore and pull out the metal from the rock. The most common method–magnetic separation–works its magic on a thick porridge of slurry moved along by water. A magnetic field operates to pull the ore particles towards a charged cylinder. The resulting aggregate of particles is referred to as a "magnetic lotus" which is in turn subject to yet more washings, spinnings, concentration and cleaning while the particles with weak magnetic force are discharged as "tailing." The iron in the earth is also what helps create our magnetic field with its poles. Hard to feel this in my kitchen even if I know it is there.

I find more vivid vocabulary as I research these industrial processes whose outcomes are the start-point for steel production. *Jaw crushers* and *stone crushers*, *a spiral classifier*, *conveyor belts* and *vibrating screens*, a *hydrocyclone* and a *dewatering tank* are all featured in the flow of raw ore to produce the concentrate that results. Iron ore processing is a major industry in India and there the tailings, high in silica content, produced in the washing process, are repurposed to make glazed ceramic tiles. I continue to be amazed by the variety of industrial outputs and ingenuity of human engineering.

At every stage of iron mining, the trucks and carts must be driven by people, the work supervised in all times of the year and conditions. Though iron ore is common throughout the globe and is the earth's fourth most abundant element, projections for running out of this resource suggest another half century will exhaust the supply.

We are at the point in the story where this rich ore, now extracted and processed, is ready to be fed into the blazing furnaces that will turn it into steel. That work turns out to be dependent on coke, a processed form of coal, that burns hot enough to drive carbon from the iron and change its physical properties. And how is coke created?

Coke production: Turning up the heat
First, any metallurgical (metal working) process needs heat. Early iron-making, for instance, depended on wood. But iron must be smelted at a high temperature and steel is produced at an even higher one. Getting a wood fire that hot is difficult. Using charcoal is one approach, but charcoal production diminishes forests rapidly, even in wood-rich environments like Brazil. So coal became the preferred source for energy in more industrialized areas. Now comes the counter-intuitive part. To increase its efficiency, a process was developed to burn coal in huge piles on the ground. The interior of these large mounds, their black smoke literally pouring off, is reduced to carbonized coal known as coke.

First developed in about the 4th century in China, coke production was only available in Britain much later, after the 17th century. Coke has even greater potential to produce heat because it is stronger and denser than the original coal. In the 19th century, the creation of coke-producing beehive ovens improved the process. These brick structures still stand in many places, sometimes in long rows of domes, other times as arched openings in a low stone wall, the dark doorways to their interior ovens silent with neglect, mute testimonies to a bygone era. Modern versions work at a much larger scale to move massive amounts of coal through a carbonization chamber.

Making coke from coal requires sustained heat over 2000 degrees Farenheit. The process known as "thermal distillation" takes eighteen to thirty-six hours in an oven, but, again, the result is a substance that can, amazingly, produce more heat than was used in its production. Coke also has the advantage that it produces very little smoke and burns very hot. Still, the coal to produce coke must be mined. Men with hard hats and heavy boots, faces grimed, ride trucks into open pits that grind the ancient organic material into chunks. Or they go into the underground shafts with lanterns and strings of lights where large drills pulverize the veins of dark black sedimentary deposits into chunks. Coal exists on every continent on earth, though the United States is particularly rich in reserves.[17] At the world's largest coal mine, in North Antelope Rochelle, Wyoming, a coal seam eighty-feet high is exposed in an open cut mine. Matte black and roughly faceted, the deposits formed between 66 and 38 million years ago as the organic material left behind in swamps and estuaries from a large inland sea were compressed from peat into carbon-rich deposits. Seen from the air, the mine is a series of dark grey geometric cuts into the organic patterns of the brown surface of the earth. Dust escapes on the wind and water run-off transports waste.

However, it turns out not just any coal will make the right coke for melting metal. A grade and quality capable of producing extreme heat for metallurgy termed "met coal" as an abbreviation is required. I can describe these processes, but I don't really know how they are done. For instance, once the coal is fed into a coke oven it sends out "coke breeze" or fumes as well as other gas and by-products. Who feeds it? How? Where do those fumes go? Learning about these processes by reading about them still leaves me without a sense of the smell, sound, heat, or any other factors involved. But I am now tangled in the thread that leads me back from steel to iron and coke to coal as essential to making my spring—and even the coke-making is not yet finished.

The coke oven has its own complexity. For instance,

Part One: Making Coffee

it includes three silicon-brick lined chambers for coking, heating, and regeneration that are all part of the "destructive" distillation process. Coke ovens are assembled in groups, known as a battery, and the vocabulary for describing the factory process includes "charging," "offtake," "door" and "quenching" emissions, a coke wharf and combustion stack as well as bunkers, conveyors, carts and pushers. Got that? I cannot say what any of those things are, how they work, who does the jobs, or what they cost.

The entire operation has a mechanistic factory aura, with echoes of 19th century industry palpably present but operating at a 21st century scale. The ovens are fed by coordinated rail carts and every step of the process is monitored on computer screens in a control room. The hot coke streams out of the ovens glowing with intense red heat and is sent off to be "quenched" with cool water. The weight of the original coal is reduced by about a quarter in the process, but the gain in energy potential is much more than the loss. The coke ovens burn constantly and turning them off, apparently, could cause damage, and so a portion of the newly made coke goes right back into this production. Strange to imagine that this self-consuming activity produces a net gain.

Not surprisingly, the work flow of coke manufacturing contains emissions and waste products at every single stage from the storage of the raw coal, which gives off particulate matter from the beginning and throughout the handling, storage, movement, and processing of the coal and coke. VOCs (volatile organic compounds) are also produced from the ovens and in the various quenching and cleaning processes. Foul gas, tar, and ammonia are exhaled by the coke oven along with naphthalene, ammonium sulfate, and hydrogen sulfide. All have been studied for "hazard identification" and their impact on animals as well as humans. Intense exposure to hydrogen sulfide leads to death. In other words, the processing of coal into coke that is just a preliminary to fueling the blast furnaces to make the steel is already fraught with filth, noise, pollution, and the accompanying byproducts of an extraction industry. The process of turning coal into coke is not self-contained. At every stage, other substances and processes are part of cleaning and refining using various oils and scrubbers along the pipeline where traveling hoods and fixed ducts are engaged to channel emissions into appropriate cleaning devices. And, of course, water is essential to various stages of cooling and cleaning. Where does it go? How is it stored or released after use?

The by-products of production are sent to various chemical plants for use in other industries (ammonium sulfate is used as a food additive in dough and as nutrient for yeast) while the coke itself is shipped to the steel mills and used to charge the blast furnaces. Our coke is now about to meet the iron ore and limestone that are essential to steel production. These have passed through a "sinter" plant where various iron ores are aggregated before they are sent to the steel mill to be turned into molten iron and slag. Sinter plants contribute major emissions in the form of dust. Though national standards exist that limit these pollutants in the United States, they are not uniformly followed.

Steel: Blasting the alloy
The oldest known steel artifact appears to be a knife from about 2100 BCE found in Turkey, forged in fire. But modern steel production generally involves a blast furnace. This technology was originally invented in China, perhaps as early as the 6th century BCE. The heart of the furnace is a cylinder of steel, lined with heat-resistant brick. The burning flames of its open maw silhouette the figures of men working in the mills—the familiar image of steel production. This primal glowing forge, alive with heat and muscular labor, imprints the blast furnace in our minds. We can readily imagine the flow of molten metal, also glowing as it runs out of the furnace and into the open molds in rivulets of bright liquid incandescent with white light.

The production of steel continues a long history in which the advantages of iron first surpassed those of bronze (an alloy of tin and copper) and were then surpassed in turn by steel. Iron work required hotter fires and higher temperatures than bronze, but gave the metal certain advantages for tools as well as weapons. Still, the real boost came with steel. Getting iron into molten form was an accomplishment—the Romans in early Britain struggled to make fires hot enough to melt the metal ore. The Iron Age involved a technological leap forward, but iron only surpasses bronze in strength if it is carbonized. The ingenuity of our ancestors remains remarkable especially considering that these ancient technologies still undergird our modern lives.

At some point, people figured out that when molten iron oxidizes, it separates into pure metal and impurities. This process reaches temperatures of over 3000 degrees Fahrenheit, though some iron will melt starting at lower temperatures. By contrast, the surface of the sun is about 10,000 degrees Fahrenheit and the magma in Kilauea is about 2200 degrees Fahrenheit—hot enough to melt most rocks. While furnaces hot enough to melt iron had been used for several millennia, the invention of blast furnaces intensified combustion through the introduction of forced air under pressure. These furnaces heat the iron to temperatures that change the properties of the metal making it stronger and more flexible. The presence of carbon gives steel its strength.

As it reaches the melting point, the liquid metal

running out from furnaces can be directed into molds and cast. Later improvements in what were known as puddling furnaces, in which the molten metal was stirred by men wielding oar-shaped instruments, removed carbon and added oxygen this is what created steel. The metal that accumulated in the "puddles" could be worked by hand, with hammers, rolled into bars or sheets.

But it was the process invented by Henry Bessemer in the mid-19th century that brought steel making into the modern age. In his method, the blast furnace makes use of air blown through molten iron to reduce the amount of carbon in the metal. The force required and the heat felt in proximity to that activity are mind-boggling. A huge furnace is fed with iron ore from the top. The heavy metal sinks, accompanied by burning coke. The fat bellied tanks of original Bessemer converters resemble an armored cylinder. Around 1952 steelmaking was improved again when pure oxygen could be pumped into the furnace to limit impurities. As these electric furnaces consume massive amounts of energy from their orifices, white hot steel pours out.

Of course, modern furnaces are far more complex than a single cylinder of brick-lined steel. The detailed list of parts would be long, but here is a list of the basic elements: blowing engines, stacks, chutes, hoppers, gas uptakes, firebrick casings, a hearth, burners, tapholes, nozzles, and a "throat" that leads into exhaust gates. In other words, a whole design and engineering industry exists to optimize steel manufacture. Nothing is simple in these processes and heat as well as pollution is part of a constant production stream. Keep in mind that we are looking at these processes just to understand what lies behind the little spring and the sharp blade in my grinder.

In steel production, energy consumption and carbon dioxide emissions are less than half of what they were a half a century ago, or so the industry claims, though it is estimated to produce about 8 per cent of all global greenhouse gas emissions. The coke used in the ovens emits a highly toxic gas already mentioned, naphthalene. Estimates are that every ton of steel produces twenty tons of liquid waste, five of waste gas, and a ton of solid waste including oxides of sulphur and carbon and emissions of fumes, acid, and dust. Most are emitted as "fugitive" products—which means they disperse rapidly—but the slags created by the industry have their own long-term slow release of graphite, soot, silica and other waste by products. The coke ovens also produce carbon-monoxide.

Again, the good news is that steel is a substance that can be almost fully recycled. Scrap steel goes back into the manufacturing process and can be effectively repurposed. Efficiencies in energy use are exemplary, the industry claims, but in comparison to what? Is their assessment simply based on monitoring the energy for the furnaces? Or does it include the full lifecycle of production? After cement, steel is one of the most mass-produced commodities, though given the amount of plastic produced in the world, that seems hard to believe.

Emissions and pollutants: Trying to come clean
Now I come across the phrase: secondary emissions. This suggests bad breath at an industrial scale, and not surprisingly, these are the biggest pollutants from steel production. These emissions and pollutants are staggering. Apparently, there are many ways to "wash" fumes produced in steel production, though the very concept is hard to grasp. The fumes contain oil mist, some visible and particulate matter, as well as volatile organic compounds (VOCs), many of which escape as "fugitive" emissions. Methods of cleaning involve "wet" and "dry" practices. The first have colorful names, like "wet cyclones" used to eliminate substances that are considered explosive, while the second involves filters and dust catchers as well as electro-static precipitators. Nice. A whole subsidiary industry has arisen just to address pollution.

The mere fact of the existence of these processes—and the image of whatever an "electro-static precipitator" might be or a "dust cake bag" filter could do—simply adds to the path by which one industrial process leads to another and another. Carbon monoxide and carbon dioxide continue to pour into the atmosphere from the tall chimneys of modern plants, simply allowed to disperse into the air. The sulfur oxides get cleansed with lime or other base chemicals and produce other byproducts. These include gypsum (which can be heat dried and used in fertilizer or for making construction material, like drywall) and ammonium sulfate, already mentioned. These processes are referred to as "desulphurization" and the general consensus among environmentalists is that scrubbing techniques are a poor approach, long-term, to dealing with

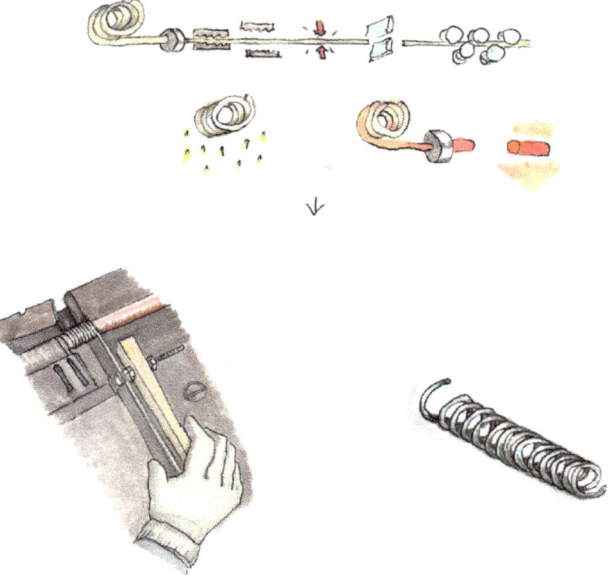

Diagram 5: The spring
Steel rods are drawn through an opening, stretching the metal and reducing its diameter into a wire. The wires are warmed and wrapped around a shaft, then heating and cooling cycles "set" the spring in its characteristic shape.

processes that should simply be improved to avoid such high levels of pollution.

The polluted water from steel production also needs extensive purification. This includes dealing with the thermal pollution as well as processing suspended matter, deadly toxins, waste acids, oil and tar, phenol, cyanide, heavy metals. Industry practices refer to such issues as emergency storage of effluents and the need for dilution facilities to be put into service in emergencies. Gas waste, iron oxide, carbon dust are among the worst problems in steel production. There are many by-products: slags, spillage muds, baghouse dusts, corrosive slags. The need for noise abatement comes into play as does attention to coping with suspended solids and run-off water. The vocabulary is vivid.

Each of these procedures involves its own specialized machinery and techniques, supply chains and transportation lines, trucking and processing costs, and all the administrative infrastructure of contemporary businesses. Due to its metal parts, my poor little coffee grinder is already complicit in multiple modes of pollution long in advance of my investigating the plastic, rubber, copper, and electricity on which it depends.

The reality is overwhelming. It occurs to me that maybe I should just acquire a stone mortar and pestle to replace my grinder.

The spring: Flexibility under stress
The steel production process described above is a global industry at an enormous scale which seems grossly disproportionate to that of the tiny spring

in my coffee grinder. Now we shift radically from these huge furnaces and their molten outputs to focus on the production of a small wire, itself produced with a whole other set of machines and procedures. Because once the steel wire is made, it still has to be processed to become a tiny spring, about the size of my thumbnail. To make this happen, the wire is warmed up to become flexible enough to wrap tightly around a shaft. Then the hot coil is dropped into oil to cool and harden, and reheated to alleviate certain structural stresses that have resulted from the coiling. Various cycles of cooling and heating are followed by a step known as "setting" the spring—compressing it so that the degree of spring is stabilized. Then the bright and shiny coil is released for work, inserted into the shaft in the plastic lid of my coffee grinder and locked in place.

All sounds fine, but I am haunted by the number of processes involved in making the spring.

Human costs: People in the process
And what of the people? The men who stand by the controls in the steel plants, who watch the ovens open, who channel the molten metal into the troughs, who breathe the smoke and fumes, whose families live nearby the mills, whose children see the steaming slag and play in the shadow of the smokestacks. All the descriptions of processes above leave

them out, as if the mills are running themselves and the interlocking parts of the system simply function seamlessly. Nothing could be further from the truth, and at every step of the way, human beings, bodies, lungs and skin are exposed. Hot and dirty physical tasks, with many risks in the everyday, expose people to hazards with other long-term cumulative effects. Photographs of the industry frequently picture the blazing furnaces and show the bright and shiny end-product reflecting light, lifted aloft or stacks in sheets and tubes, as if it simply rolled off a conveyor belt, magically perfected in a pristine environment.

When a steel mill was built in Brazil in the 1940s, the men who cleared the forest were barefooted, climbing on the fallen trunks and walking through the cut branches without shoes. Workers in the mills were promised one shoe on signing a contract, a second on showing up for work. The nationally sponsored project created the entire village of Volta Redonda in the jungle, in the Paríba Valley, with housing and schools, a church and playing fields.

The picture has a darker side. Heart rate variability is known to increase in the vicinity of the mills. Asthma cases shoot sky high in Pittsburgh. Childhood asthma rates are three times that of the national average in steel towns. Mortality rates for those over sixty-five are statistically higher in steel towns than elsewhere in similarly aged populations—and these are simply residents, not the workers who have more intense exposure to pollutants. Employment rules and danger notices (in multiple languages) were posted in the 20th century in the mills in the United States. The work was hard, hot, and much of the time, in the coal mines the opposite, it was damp and cold.[18] But the jobs were good jobs in the days when the wages of workers, while much lower than that of management, still provided a living.

Steelworkers' unions were formed in the 1930s. Working conditions were gradually regulated so that hours, pay, and safety improved. But in 2021, steelworkers in five states went on strike against the conglomerate Brackenridge. The workers had had no raises in seven years. The company had cut the number of employees, increased shift hours, and passed on health care costs to their workers while increasing production in high profit margin areas—steel for aerospace—and decreasing it in others.

When I press a small smooth button on the lid of my coffee grinder where I feel the spring push back, the action connects me to this history and contemporary strife, struggle, and pollution.

Part One: Making Coffee

The blade: Cold metal, sharp edge
The blade in my grinder is also steel, die stamped from rolled sheets produced through the same industrial processes just described. The machine rooms in which these actions are performed are filled with huge powerful stamping presses. These are several times the weight of the human beings who operate them, standing at the bed of the presses as the die comes down under pressure heavy enough to cut out the shapes from the steel. The sound on the factory floor resonates with the pounding crush of the weight of the power press. The human operator still manipulates the material, slipping it under the die cutter and pulling it out.

The machines are heavy, oily, and are lined up along the aisles of the factory with wide storage palettes stacked beside them to receive the newly shaped metal pieces. The presses have a primal machine look to them, bulky and unwieldy, heavy and solid. The operators stand at their posts throughout their shifts, performing repetitive motions. Skills required for these positions involve expertise in using calipers, micrometers, and rulers, ability to drive and manipulate a forklift, skill in evaluating raw materials and finished products, and a host of other related abilities. The average pay in the industry is between $15.00-$21.00 an hour. Over half of the steel stamping plants in the United States are in Ohio, Michigan, and Illinois. What is it like to live in those states on a salary of between $30,000 and $42,000 a year? Raise a family?

The hazards of the work are physical as much as chemical. Exposure to operating parts of heavy machines increases the risk of injury—as does inadequate or improper training. Additional risks come from electricity operated under unsafe conditions where workers are not provided with personal protective equipment. While metal fabrication produces fewer hazardous wastes than many other industrial metal production, it still creates by products such as spent metalwork fluid or wastewater, often contaminated with oil and grease. In the metal stamping or forming process, some of the metalworking fluid evaporates as mist. Metal chips, oily rags, and fugitive emissions—all contribute to the dissemination of toxins into air, water, eyes, lungs, and onto the skin.

Workers at the stamping presses wear gloves that cause their hands to sweat throughout the shift, damaging the barrier property of skin and creating susceptibility to infection or irritant contact dermatitis. Engine oil and petroleum products are known carcinogens, and repeated use of vibrating mechanisms has an adverse effect on hands and arms. The inhalation of mist from evaporating metalworking fluids is associated with work-related asthma, a significant health risk in many industries and a contributor to healthcare costs and workman's compensation claims.[19] The weary worker at the end of the shift coughs while commuting home, eyes burning, arms shaking, and lungs compromised. On the carefully organized palette next to the press, the shiny, newly-cut blades of my coffee grinder have been neatly stacked for shipping and assembly. Their silence reveals nothing of their manufacture.

The blade will still need shaping and sharpening. But where by whom? I find a company advertising itself as a source for "specialty blades" for any purpose or industry through techniques that are entirely controlled by computer-driven machinery that allows them to create unique and purpose-specific razor-sharp edges of all kinds with unprecedented precision.[20] More machines that make parts for other machines...

Diagram 6: Rubber gaskets

Organic rubber comes from trees which are cut each morning so their sap runs and is collected and processed, washed and poured through screens and sieves to remove debris. Synthetic rubber is produced from crude oil processing (not shown) and then processed into sheets and chunks. Waste water and byproducts exude fumes and toxins. The rubber material gets cut and molded into custom shapes for a wide variety of purposes.

Gaskets and rings: The soft rubber parts
A few more of the grinder's parts are also calling for our attention: rubber nipples, gaskets, collars, and rings that cushion and diminish vibration play their own role in the operation of my little appliance. Tracking the manufacture of its other parts has already worn me out. But vibration isolation and noise reduction are essential if ear-splitting sounds are not to be produced by the daily operation of my grinder. The history of rubber is connected with global expansion and colonialism as Europeans arrived in the New World and discovered novel products and materials. For instance, Christopher Columbus is rumored to have been intrigued by the sight of a ball bouncing when he watched a group of indigenous peoples playing an unfamiliar game. Rubber did not exist in the European environment. Not much bounced in the old world but babies on knees.

Among the Olmecs, credit for the discovery is given to a woman who saw trees crying, oozing a white sap from their bark. Natural latex, boiled and shaped, had great properties of resilience in addition to being the way the trees healed themselves after an injury. Originally found only in Brazil and South American, the rubber tree was spread by the British and Europeans. Both French and British geographers saw the benefit of the plant and brought seeds to Europe in the 18th century. A British traveler, Henry Wickham, is reputed to have smuggled around 70,000 seeds from Brazil and put them in the ground in Kew Gardens where a small percentage of them germinated. These plants were then used by the British spread to rubber to Southeast Asia—Indonesia, Singapore, Malaysia and other areas where the climate was well-suited to their growth.

Huge and highly productive rubber plantations grew up as part of colonial enterprises. Labor practices were violent and abusive. In many places, workers were forced to toil. Torture, murder, and mutilation were common. In the 1920s Henry Ford created a whole village in the Amazon, Fordlândia, as part of his zealous efforts to export ideology while exploiting indigenous workers. His project failed and was abandoned by 1934. The ruins of the Brazilian-American villages–water tower, warehouses, and other buildings—remain standing in a state of abandonment.

Rubber plantations still exist in many former colonies, their lean long trees elegantly spaced in straight lines, creating a light canopy above the planted lines. A recent report by a United Nations Mission to the nation of Liberia contained a long list of concerns about nearly every aspect of the industry. Handling of the rubber, lack of protective gear, chemicals used, waste disposal, drinking water, the conditions in living quarters and the clinic, latrines, maintenance shops for generators, fuel storage—in other words, every facet of the operation is fraught. The management of current plantations keeps the workers ignorant of risks and does not address environmental protection or safety standards.

Workers living on plantations get their drinking water from a shallow stream.[21] The health clinic on site had no electricity or trained staff. This is now. This is not a snapshot from a hundred or fifty years ago. The job of the workers is to wound the trees, cutting them with tools so they bleed latex through a spout in their trunks. Many of these workers are children. The trees are tapped in the morning and the latex gathered in the afternoon. As with any process of raw material extraction, the sequence of steps involved in going from the trees to the final product in my coffee grinder's parts involves many processes such as coagulation, chemical treatments, water, baths, cleaning, along with specialized machinery and many additives.

Synthetic rubber production has increased dramatically. The process was spurred in part by a mid-20th century shutdown of supply chains when Japan closed the access to rubber plantations in South East Asia during conflicts of the Second World War. Synthetic rubber is created from oil and coal turned into a compound that has the wonderful properties of "elastic deformation"—stretching, squishing, shape shifting—and rebound. The polymer based substance, SBR (styrene-butadiene rubber), is used to make tires, flooring, cushioning, and almost all other materials that claim the name "rubber." In other words, it is like nearly everything else in industrial manufacturing, a product of fossil remains and their carbons.

But what are we doing? Synthetic rubber is completely non-biodegradable. Completely. Organic rubber, by contrast, can be recycled and reused quite effectively. Odds are very much against my coffee grinder's gaskets and noise reduction parts being made of organic rubber since seals, belts, and industrial items are almost all made of synthetic rubber.

As in the case with other industries, the publicity for rubber manufacturing plants shows bright and shiny vats, silos, and tanks. The refinement of raw materials, oil and coal, occurs out of sight in the polished workings of the elaborate machinery. Highly flammable naptha is one of the main by-products of crude oil processing, and must be handled very carefully when it is combined with other gases to make the basic building blocks of synthetic rubber molecules. Additional chemical agents are used to cause these molecules to bond and form "substances" or the basic soup that can be further subjected to a process called "Vulcanisation." Here the ancient god of fire and the forge returns, as the rubber material is subjected to heat and sulfur to give it greater elasticity as well as hardness. The sulfur? From volcanic areas, mined, processed, and subject to its own series of industrial procedures.

Online, I find an industry video full of exquisite images. Synthetic chunks of rubber in close-up have the consistency of high-end whale blubber, white and creamy. Huge mounds of it fluffed on the factory floor look like pure cumulus clouds rising into atmospheric splendor. It responds to the touch with a smooth elasticity, springing back into form, as demonstrated in the promotional video. The documentary stresses the computerized control of the manufacturing process directed by a single operator at a console of screens that provide views of a puffertank, expeller, and other machines functioning without the presence of humans. Solvents and raw materials are stored in large vats with elaborate piping and venting systems, an engineer's dream of seamless efficiency. Again, the industry promotes an image of laboratory conditions, controlled reactions between catalysts and raw substances. The liquid mixture is stirred constantly until the right moment for it to coagulate—always in accord with the specific task for which the rubber is being prepared—tires, hoses, cushioning, casting and so on. In the intermediate step, the rubber is kept moving in water, a collection of small white beads formed for multiple purposes.

Water gushes through the process, used for transport as well as cooling until the "crumbs" as the beads are known are shaken on a conveyor belt that functions as a sieve. Pressed to remove more water, tested for quality, the beads are then sent through another set of tubes where hot air helps to dry the rubber before it is compressed into bales. These semi-translucent solid blocks look like lard or wax, ready to be used.

The rubber parts in my grinder are small, cast rubber, made by pushing the raw liquid of synthetic polymers into a mold in a manner just like that of the gas valve in the coffee bean bag. The vocabulary for describing the parts of the rubber molding process is again suggestive, a whole universe of specialized references to the ram, mold cavity, tear trim beads, flash pad and transfer pot. So each tiny piece of the grinder links to another series of industrial processes, specific parts, manufacturing of the machines that make the parts, and these machines, in turn, are the outcome of elaborate industries. The realization continues to be overwhelming. And all we have dealt with so far is the spring mechanism and the blade. We have not even glanced at the casing or the motor. We still have a long way to go.

The lid: Hard plastics
As if that PET were not enough plastic, we now turn to the polypropylene resin used to make the lid of the coffee maker, the second most common plastic and therefore also produced in massive quantities. Like most plastics currently in production, the lid and casing are petroleum products. Sigh. These plastics are polymers, which is to say, they are chemical compounds whose structure makes them highly versatile, resistant to breakage, heat, and cold, and capable of being shaped and molded into a nearly infinite number of forms. This is a different kind of plastic from the PET film used in producing the bag for the coffee beans, harder and more heat resistant. I continue to be amazed by the number of ways human beings have managed to reorganize the chemistry of the material world into substances that serve so many specific purposes.

Part One: Making Coffee 113

The polypropylene industry is worth billions and billions of dollars worldwide. Like all plastic production, it involves industrial processes at a large scale that begin with pumping oil from the earth, transporting it by land and sea using more fossil fuels, then transforming it through heat, chemistry, and physical means until the output is a kind of pellet that can be used to make pretty much anything that has a three-dimensional form. In this case, that is the translucent plastic lid on which I have put pressure every morning for decades grinding my beans.

Depending on the specific chemical structure, the plastic will have different properties, but the generic process for making the lid is the same as that of many common objects in our everyday lives from chairs to clothes to construction materials as well as small household items. The process was first developed by Phillips Petroleum researchers in the early 1950s and made commercially viable at a large scale by an Italian firm, Montecatini a few years later. That company began as a small mining operation in a hill town in Tuscany in the 1880s, a fact that has almost no bearing on my coffee grinder, except that the history of its emergence as a quasi-monopoly for chemical production in Europe in the early 20th century led to this innovation in plastics. The photographs of the hill town show its medieval profile, like a picture perfect image in an illuminated manuscript.

While it is a truism to state that plastics changed modern life, the more profound impact is rarely stated as clearly—that the use and production of plastics has changed the very force and energy of life itself. The living-ness of the planetary ecosystems is bound to the changes wrought by these massive industries. The lid to my coffee grinder is a tiny miniscule and utterly insignificant item in this larger picture, except that it both embodies and represents another major industry of extraction, production, and pollution. According to a report by the Center for International Environmental Law (CIEL), "In 2019 alone, the production and incineration of plastic will add more than 850 million metric tons of greenhouse gases to the atmosphere—equal to the pollution from 189 new 500-megawatt coal-fired power plants."[22]

Can the environmental cost of the lid of my coffee grinder be justified by spreading it across the decades of its use, or should I repent and acquire a hand grinder, made of metal blades and a wooden base with a drawer for the newly ground beans? Or stop buying anything at all? The image of the mortar and pestle rises again. I'm done with the lid.

The motor: From charge to spin
In addition to the polished steel grinding chamber, blades, and springs, the coffee grinder consists of a hard plastic casing around a small electric motor. The motor is the outcome of applied physics in the modern age. You could even argue that these motors are what made modernity possible, shifting from animal, wind, and water power to ubiquitous electricity.

I've never stopped to think about how a motor works. I just figured you plug it in, turn it on, and it spins. But as it turns out, every electric motor depends on magnetism. My grinder motor has two magnets in it and the opposition of their polarities creates a force. When that is crossed by a flowing electric current it produces a vector force that can be harnessed for mechanical energy. What? Yes, the tension between the magnetic field and one created by the current that flows into the motor with electricity makes the force that spins the stator and rotor elements, brushes, axles and other parts. I find this truly remarkable.

The electric current that charges through the motor is another player in modern life. In the conducting material of copper, the stodgy protons stay in place, bound to the nucleus of their atoms, while electrons create a charge that can be carried through the wire coil. The electrons get into an excited state—who wouldn't with a jolt of current? The atomic interactions are not mechanical. No little train of electrons is shuffling along through the wire. Instead they vibrate, producing a wave of energy at a certain frequency and amplitude. A wave moves through a medium, this case, copper wire, but the electrons do not travel. Electrons are hyperactive and very sensitive to magnetic forces, drawn as they are towards positive poles. Far below the level of my perception, these profound actions are taking place every time I press the lid to connect the current to activate the motor.

My small grinder uses one of the four major forces in the universe, magnetism, in a process researched by 19th-century figures like Michael Faraday and James Clerk Maxwell, who were fascinated by electromagnetism and its properties. When I look up the design of the most basic electric motor, I am struck by the ingenuity of these scientist-engineers. Weirdly enough, if the magnets in my grinder were allowed to move freely, suspended in water or air, they would line up with the north and south magnetic poles of the earth, just like a compass needle. But the force of their charge is not strong enough to will them towards that behavior as long as they are mounted in the motor and in the grinder's plastic casing. The grinder does not rotate on its own on my counter top to align with the earth's magnetic field. Still the technological alchemy of ordinary life is shot through with unnoticed dimensions.

The electrical cord plugs into the outlet, also a familiar form of flexible molded plastic with its two metal prongs, snaking into place. The standardization of electrical systems renders their details invisible. What other form would an electrical cord take but this one? Different adapters for standards exist around the globe, as any traveler knows. But in all cases, once the plug is connected to a power source the charge pulses through the wire in a steady stream of energy transfer. Imagine, electrical energy is waiting, latent, available, at every outlet in your home, office, factory, or laboratory.

My initial reaction to seeing an image of a motor for a coffee grinder is that it looks like a little robot part, with a bright wire, shiny copper wire bundles, and an assemblage of machined elements put together into a highly specific and complex whole. The motor parts have exotic names like "brush housing" and "stator coil" and the descriptions of their functions are equally suggestive "constrains part X" or "provides" or "enhances" magnetic poles. Torque and other mechanical effects are produced by this compact motor which rests on the base plate of the grinder unit, neatly sealed away. Getting access to the motor in my grinder would take some doing. A trigger button, wires, and multiple contact points have soldered the motor so it stays in place. Steel aluminum, and copper are all combined in what is classified as a "single phase" half-horsepower motor. Again, the single job of the motor is to transform electromagnetism into motion, or, to transform one form of energy (electrical) into another (mechanical).

The rotor moves. The stator does not. That makes sense, given their names. But the mystery of electricity remains profound, and the idea that I have a small engine generating a magnetic field on my kitchen counter is further evidence of how much once-experimental applied knowledge has become inconspicuously integrated into daily life.

I can't follow all the details of the design of the electrical parts, the way the wire current cuts across coils wound around a magnet, or precisely how the magnetic circuit is generated. What I do know is that what is visible when the small motor is removed from the grinder are the bright coils of copper wire as well as the many other components of the rotor, the shaft, the bearings, and the pulley drive that transfers the motor rotation to the physical/mechanical components of the blade assembly. Reflect on these multiple actions, consider that a pulley is a fundamental physical device, one whose actions were the subject of high school physics. This is a mechanical device, used by human beings since antiquity. But the motor is a modern feature, the outcome of centuries of scientific innovation. Benjamin Franklin may have captured electricity in a glass like a luminous living animal, but it could not be tamed and used in a systematic way until the 19th century.

All that past history underpins my invisible motor, the sound and feel of which has a satisfying hum and buzz. The detailed design of both stator and rotor spins us back into the realm of metal working, iron, but also copper. Copper, that strategic element of the ancient world, was mined in Cyprus (which takes its name from the metal) by about 4000 BC. This gave the island a crucial position in the economics and culture of the Mediterranean. Now Chile is the world's largest supplier of copper, with mines in Peru, Indonesia, and Mexico also contributing huge supplies. In the United States, Arizona is one supplier of copper, and its mines supply ore that is rapidly processed into wire in nearby plants.

I wonder if the transformation of copper rod to wire is similar to that of steel in the little spring. It begins with bold, shiny rods, thick geometric forms extruded into long bars. They are ingots, poured molten into their solid form. Copper, bright and reflective, is hardly altered at all from its original chemical state—so lively are its electrons that they produce a highly conductive substance. The electrons move with ease and have such a free path that they collide infrequently and therefore their resistance to electrical currents is low. Figure that out?

Copper, a pretty red-gold metal, is attractive to humans for decoration as well as other purposes. It used to be produced in separate lengths that had to be butt-welded into longer wires. Now a process called continuous casting allows for the wire to be produce in long rolls. These are then subjected to the same "wire-drawing" as aluminum or steel, by which the malleable material is pulled through a die, reducing the diameter as the metal stretches into a fine filament of desired dimensions. Copper, like other raw materials, is extracted from the earth. At the mines this creates acidic mists that harm skin and eyes and lungs as well as destroying crops and even damaging the surfaces of buildings nearby. Hard to see this in the bright red shining metal.

The specialized vocabulary of all the rest of the parts in the motor points to the particular lifecycles of production: iron plates, a rotor coil, main shaft, copper brush, and bearings. The bearings and small washers are made of steel as are various pieces like brackets and housing that hold the motor components in place. Other bits and pieces are made of plastic, such as the housing that keeps the motor in place. Switch leads and safety papers, a power cord retention clip, internal motor gasket and power cord reel—the list goes on and on, but I cannot follow all these individual bits and pieces into their lifecycles without becoming crazy.

Outer Casing: The hard shell
In this ongoing investigation, we have looked at coffee beans and their lifecycle, the bag in which they were packaged, and some of the components of the coffee grinder—spring, blade, plastic lid and motor. Now I turn my attention to the outer casing, opaque white plastic. What possible mysteries could be concealed in such an apparently innocuous element?

The casing is made of hard plastic, which insulates the motor and its moving parts, keeps the blade and grinding chamber safe from stray fingers. It is infused with dyes and color so that it can be matched to contemporary décor. Made through the process of injection molding, it is designed to absorb impact without cracking. Injection molding, which we have visited before with the bag valve, sounds straightforward enough. Take a nice soft plastic material and shoot it into a cavity so it can take the shape of the mold. But nothing is that simple. The production takes place at an industrial site.

Part One: Making Coffee 121

Photographs of these thermoplastic plants are replete with shiny, wiped clean aluminum surfaces, fluorescent lights, catwalks and scaffolding with conveyor belts and elaborate tubing connected with gauges and wires and components running on smoothly flanged wheels. In other words, a whole future-is-now high-tech automated-seeming world of clean production that is actually not clean at all.

I plunge into industry publications full of descriptions of fast-clamping molds and instructions for resin drying as well as global partnerships for high-quality recycled materials. Thermoplastic composites contain "flow additives" and even bioplastics. Some are sugar based and made with lubricating agents that have high levels of food-contact compliance. Sounds so easy. The elaboration of specialized features goes on and with it an endless proliferation of vocabulary. Photographs of these components are all pristine, beautifully lit, so that they sparkle and glow with the light of seamlessly perfect production. The operators of the shiny apparatus are out of sight, and when present, are often depicted in lab coats and goggles, pseudo-scientists performing in these perfect super-clean workplaces. All human presence is erased in favor of showcasing the technology.

Injection molding makes use of materials common to all plastics—the natural materials are coal, cellulose, salt, crude oil, and natural gas, as we have already seen. These are all processed into a basic substance that can be put to a wide range of purposes. Thermoplastics, which can be repeatedly melted by heating and then solidified when they cool, are considered completely recyclable on account of this versatility. But, of course, all plastics used for injection molding release toxic fumes and vapors in the process.

Now, let's just picture the moments in which the grinder casing is made. In an industrial plant, an operator approaches a funnel-like hopper in a machine. Suddenly they realize that bright blue plastic granules were used for the last job. Since this plastic casing is going to be white, the operator purges the system at a high temperature with chemical agents that produce bitter fumes and smoke in the work area. The injection area overheats and sharp, acrid odors of hydrogen chloride, styrene, nitrogen, and cyanide permeate the air. The operator coughs, choking slightly in what is medically described as a laryngeal spasm.

As the day wears on, a slight headache sets in, accompanied by a bit of dizziness. On bad days, they have a sense of confusion and a slight unsteadiness to their gait. As the operator removes the mold from the cavity for making my grinder casing, a tiny cloud of particulate matter puffs into the air while the release agents that help loosen the mold give off a small smoke plume. All of this evaporates while the operator works. Over time, work in the industry produces kidney damage and decreased lung function that contributes to the chances of developing chronic respiratory problems.[23]

My grinder has lasted more than twenty years. In that time, what has happened to the operator who managed the machine the day it was made? Hoods for capturing fumes and particulate matter help mitigate these effects when they are installed properly in the work environment. The exposure to cyanide has probably the most severe effects and can result in convulsions, coma, and death. If you read the medical analysis of what cyanide does, you find that it interferes in the processing of oxygen in the bloodstream at the cellular level. Needless to say, that is a fatal effect.

The production of the grinder casing repeats other plastic material lifecycles. In addition, there are the dyes or pigments that make it white—usually a titanium based substance that imparts brightness and opacity to the plastic.[24] These are known carcinogenic substances and dangerous when inhaled. Titanium dioxide occurs in nature, and one large source is the Ries crater in Bavaria. Interestingly, this is an impact crater formed by a meteorite believed to have hit about 14 million years ago. Apollo astronauts discovered a related compound, ilmenite, in lunar rocks as well, though on earth it was formed as igneous rock cooled slowly in magma chambers. Ilmenite is black, shiny, and processed to produce fine grained black sand. But, curiously, it also provides the source from which the titanium ore can be extracted to create a bright white highly-reflective substance. Ground to a powder it is widely used as a pigment in all kinds of materials. The moon rocks in which it was found are old—nearly three billion years—and have a higher percentage of titanium dioxide than the rocks found on earth. But I do not think any moon dust has found its way into my grinder casing.

So there it is. The brilliant white titanium is associated with increased risk of cancer, and is also frequently a cause of inflammation when used in tooth whitening agents or implants. As I am unlikely to pulverize my grinder casing and put it in my mouth, the odds are relatively small that it will cause me harm in its current state, but if I backtrack through the entire production process, I am again in the realm of extraction where large earth-moving machines and men with shovels produce air filled with dust in regions as far away as the other side of the world—with China and Russia as the top producers. In the Ural mountains, where vast concentrations of precious ores and metals reside, the Trans-Siberian railway passes through areas of fast flowing streams, evergreen forests and mountains filled with traditional wooden architecture, churches, monasteries, the first burial site of the remains of the last Russian Emperor Nicholas II and his family, and even Neolithic rock paintings. Could that dramatically beautiful landscape be where my grinder pigment was sourced?

I will probably never know where the titanium in my plastic came from, or even know for sure, without forensic testing, that it is this mineral that colors the casing. But by some similarly complex path, that material has come to sit on my counter in the innocuous but smooth form of the coffee grinder cast to fit my hand and reliably serve its purpose. If I were to filter the wind in my neighborhood, catch the breeze that rifles the leaves of the sycamore tree in my yard and rattles the pine cones free from the redwood, would I be able to detect grains of particulate matter distributed from these remote and not-so-remote areas of the globe to which I am attached by transmission lines of manufacture? Do I ever, inadvertently, inhale that powdered ilmenite or titanium in raw form as a minute presence among the other powdered substances in the air?

The Power Cord: The chemical threat
To track the lifecycle of the power cord and its prongs, we could go halfway around the globe, though possibly my cord was created closer to home. A strong young woman, arms bare to the elbow, wearing a regulation uniform in bright worker blue moves her hands around the moving parts of a shiny machine. She is fully focused, her concentration palpable, as she watches the action. We are in Yaroslavl, Russia, in a factory where almost all the workers are women, all in standard issue blue uniforms whose sleeves are edged with cheerful striped cuffs.[25] All have their hair cut short or tied back, most wear gloves, and sit at their workstations with concentrated attention.

The materials they are assembling have already been through the many stages of raw material extraction, processing, and formation into what becomes power cords through pressurizing and molding. The machines in the factory are brightly colored, their blue and green enamel-baked coatings creating a cheerful atmosphere. The long days of repetitive work may or may not be enlivened by the green linoleum on the floor or worktable, but the scale of this power cord factory is intimate by contrast to the scenes of steel production or copper wire making described earlier. The rooms are lit by long large windows and the women use bare hands and work without masks. The tasks are fussy rather than dangerous, requiring handwork to cut the long cords into lengths, strip the insulation from the wires as they are fitted into the plugs.

Before these Russian women can perform their work assembling the cords, many industrial processes have already taken place—creation of the copper rods transformed into filament through the drawing process already described. The copper wire used in the cords is annealed, a heating process that strengthens the wires and keeps them from oxidizing. Who does that? Where? And with what equipment? The conducting wire is created from multiple strands of monofilament, to produce a more flexible and stronger cord. The outer sheath of flexible plastic provides insulation. For every step in the process, specialized equipment is manufactured—from a three-flat pin plug crimping machine to one that performs automatic braiding or twist-weaving of copper filament.

Once again, to account for this equipment requires a long account of extraction and processing of metals— steel and aluminum—and the machines that process the copper and so on would be required.

The outer layer of the cord, once made of rubber, is now a polymer coating made of PVC (polyvinyl chloride), Teflon, or polyethylene, all components we have already encountered in other plastic parts of the coffee grinder. PVC is mainly made of salt and oil, which is to say, it is a product of the petrochemical industry. The petroleum is subjected to extreme heat in steam furnaces which transforms the molecular structure. The different components in the liquid can be segmented and then captured individually. For PVC, ethylene and chlorine are essential. A series of what are termed "thermal cracking" processes are used to combine the ethylene with the chlorine into a form that is sent through another reactor that makes the molecules bond with each other. More chemistry at industrial scale.

This all sounds very laboratory safe and hygienic until you find out that Greenpeace considers PVC the single most poisonous plastic and the one that contributes the most damaging pollution through the production and disposal cycles.[26] The worst part? The chlorine. Chlorine is now present everywhere in the food chain through its presence in water and air. A known carcinogen, it disrupts hormones and causes damage to the immune system. PVC production contributes about 40% of the chlorine in the United States. But a statement like that does nothing to emphasize the dramatic reality that chlorine is a basic contributor to monstrous products and disastrous events—Agent Orange, Love Canal, DDT–on account of dioxin contamination. This is a by-product created when chlorine-based products are made. Burning PVC in any waste site, or accident, releases huge amounts of dioxins which, once inhaled, remain in the body in measurable amounts.

As is too common in these industries, the location of the plants where chlorine is processed are in Texas and Louisiana, in other words, in poor rural areas with vulnerable populations. Accounts exist of entire towns too polluted to sustain—such as Reveilletown, Louisiana, where, again according to Greenpeace, every structure including the church and homes of over a hundred residents was torn down. The Dow chemical company sometimes buys out a town and relocates its population because of contamination.

But it is the direct off-gassing of PVC—the new car smell, the transfer from cling wrap, and release of chemicals from mini-blinds or other domestic products—that makes it so pervasive. In a fire the substance becomes a gas so lethal that attempts are being made to prevent its use in construction. So, the innocuous and familiar power cord on my grinder is part of a cycle of toxin production that has infiltrated the global systems affecting the reproduction of wildlife, created deformities and brain damage, and contributed to the very attention deficit disorder that itself results in ever more ignorance about and disregard for these effects.

In spite of the many warnings about these impacts, advocacy campaigns have not stopped the increase in PVC production—which is now the third most popular synthetic plastic in the world. Taiwan and Japan lead the production with thousands of kilotons of output a year. But the United States, China, the United Kingdom and Mexico are all major players. How can this ever change? The investment in the infrastructure that creates the processes and supply chains is vast and our dependence—or perceived dependence—on the constant manufacture of new goods and products is overwhelming. I leave the grinder plugged in, and don't think of the many roads that lead to the power cord, its smooth outer surface so totally within the norm of modern life I cannot manage to look at it as the outcome of horrific evils, the contributor to the death of wildlife, and damage to children and vulnerable populations.[28]

• •

Paper filter: From forest to trash
I pull an unbleached coffee filter from the drawer and it is soft as a napkin to my touch. Clean and fresh, crimped on its edges, it opens gracefully as it is pinched and slides into the cone of the coffee maker. A perfect fit, its inside seams are ready to hold the grounds and water. I cannot imagine the number of design and production decisions behind this inconspicuous filter.

To begin with, the filter paper is made from a specific long fiber designed to allow only certain sizes of particles to pass through when wet. What? Yes, for the filter to let brewed coffee flow into the canister below, it doesn't just keep the grounds separate as they swell with hot water, it discretely manages the amount of coffee bean in the drink. Oh.

In the coffee industry, the filter is gauged according to a wide range of specifications. These assess its *compatibility*, *efficiency*, and *capacity*. The first quality defines its ability to deal with heat and chemical conditions, the second the rate at which it retains particles of varying sizes, and the last is the balance between that retention and the flow permitted. A highly designed object, not just any random cone of folded paper, the coffee filter has its own lifecycle and history. Needless to say, it also connects to multiple industries, production processes, supply chains, and life-cycles which we will look at now in turn.

Consider the paper pulp, often taken from fast-growing trees like Loblolly Pine and Hybrid Aspen. The paper industry is so detailed in its management that it produces estimates on how many hours per acre it takes to grow fiber for paper. For instance, one estimate suggests that enough commercial pulpwood to make 4,000 reams of office paper could be grown in one year on 100 acres.[29] But of course, growing the trees is only part of the story. The trees have to be planted, brought to their rapid maturity, and harvested. Each of these phases of the life-cycle requires specialized labor and equipment organized in highly coordinated systems within seasonal patterns related to the geographical location where the trees are planted. Here we go again.

The euphemistic generalization "forest industries" covers a host of practices which are often fraught with ecological costs. For instance, a form of tree-related VOC—volatile organic compound—is created by intensified tree farming. While many VOCs are human-made, biogenic (BVOC) versions are also prevalent, vaporize rapidly, and pose health risks.[30] We think of trees as participating in carbon capture, and in producing oxygen. But in areas of concentrated increases in forest plantations, VOC emissions have also grown dramatically. Some are produced by drying and pressing, actions essential for making wood composites. Biogenic VOCs are produced by the plants as part of their growth, reproduction, and communication systems. Intensifying tree growth concentrates the biogenic VOC levels in a region even without burning or processing the lumber. So it seems that overcrowding turns out to be a problem in many species.

Diagram 7 (right): The paper filter

Paper made from wood begins with logging, selecting trees, cutting them with power tools, and transporting them from the forest site. The logs are stripped of their bark and then chipped to be used in the paper making process which includes massive beaters and pulping machines. The wet pulp is turned into a continuous roll of paper which is then die-cut and crimped. The paper box in which the filters are packed is also die cut and printed before being folded into shape to serve as packaging.

Part One: Making Coffee   133

When I begin to look, I find that every step of paper production involves industrial activities that cause pollution and waste. These include specialized equipment and treatments that are part of longer lifecycles of production. The original limbs taken from a pine tree, for instance, must be sent into "a "de-barking drum"" to remove their outer covering. Then the remains are sent to a chipper. These statements are so bland that they hide the smell of pine resin, the sound of chain saws and choppers, the manufacture of a heavy metal drum that performs the act of stripping bark from the still living wood, its soft wet sap running and freshly peeled limbs sweet and young, their pale-pink flesh laid bare. The chipper works at an industrial scale. The output fills an entire warehouse of wood chips in which the loose piles of ochre-brown flakes reach to the ceiling. The smell is sweet, but the air is full of particulate matter that clogs the lungs from the drying chips.

Wood fiber is tough. Turning it into paper pulp requires massive energy for beating. In commercial paper production, this involves enormous cookers, boilers, beaters, piping and water, electricity and exhaust. The site where this takes place is once again a scene of metal vats linked to energy supplies. The list of different components of the pulping process, taken from a supplier's site, is daunting. Here are a few of the machine types listed, just for pulping: super batch cooking, gravity disc thickener, single screw

Part One: Making Coffee

press, twin roll press, continuous cooking system, displacement cooking digesters—the list goes on. The details of the process involve multiple chemical reactions and physical actions. Images in the industry always show the machines without human operators, except in rare cases where they appear in lab coats and apparently clean, hygienic, sterile environments and safe work places.

But let's backtrack into the forest briefly to follow more details of the logging process. Imagine teams of workers involved in transforming living trees into material to be stripped and pulped. Heavy equipment operators do the logging and drive the trucks. No tree comes down without human labor. Climbing massive trees with cleats and belts, carrying a chain saw to trim limbs that fall to the ground below, being hoisted aloft in a basket while letting out rope are all parts of the routine. And on days when it rains and is cold, damp, wet—what then? What are the occupational hazards in the logging industry? Injuries to life and limb.

Each tree has to be identified, cut skillfully to fall just right, then its limbs stripped off to optimize the load on the flatbed truck. Calculating the direction of the fall is an art, as is using an earth mover to clear a landing spot. Putting raw, fresh-cut trees onto the truck and securing the load, men in hardhats operate a bull-dozer with huge calipers that pick the logs up in their jaws and swing them into place aligned with the length of the truck's body. Bulldozers use diesel fuel at a cost of about $5/hour, and emission from these motors contributes to background air pollution through exhaust that contains nitrogen oxide and particulate matter. Nitrogen oxide is an ingredient in ground-level ozone and is associated with respiratory problems and lung damage. Particulate matter is linked to premature mortality. "Premature mortality" is a euphemism that means death at a young age.

This is just the beginning. We haven't even gotten the newly logged trees out of the forest yet. The trucks also run on diesel, hauling the logs to the site of processing. Earth moving and bulldozing equipment make significant contributions to pollution despite increased regulations on non-road diesel engine operation. Mechanics, maintenance planners, millwrights, and technicians skilled at every kind of machine and electrical system, steamfitters and pipefitters, vibration analysts, and even the occasional silviculture (forest management) experts with knowledge of wood and trees are all part of the forest industry in the landscape, mill, and factory.

I find an industry diagram that shows a stand of trees and then a bark stripping drum followed by a little chipper. This cartoon does not document the paper producing lifecycle. Reducing these processes to discrete steps as if they lead without interruption from one to another, magically, only deflects the reality and complexity of fume producing exhalations and risks of human exposure at every risky step. Sadly, my diagrams also do this.

Also, the processes are not uniform for every kind of wood, and the paper filter is produced from fast-growing softwood, pine, pulped by a slightly different method than in harder woods. Soft woods have longer fibers, which are good for making coffee filters that are permeable. Suddenly, we are in the realm of biochemistry as a basis for paper production. I find out that the wood chips have to be cooked under high pressure to separate the basic cellulose from lignin, which is a structural element in cell walls and plant tissues. Ok. That is because the cellulose is the softer fiber that lends itself to repurposing as pulp. Processing wood fiber involves heat, water, various chemicals, and a host of recycling to take the spent chemistry and turn it into something useful through another process of recovery that allows many of the chemicals and by products to be repurposed as fuel to keep the cycle going. The estimate is that it takes ten liters (about two and a half gallons) of water to produce one sheet of standard office paper. Estimates are that Americans use more than eighty-two gallons of water a day—equivalent to the weight of two adult pandas.[31] But the water used in paper making is often diverted from communities, used, and returned in contaminated form so that local populations, including indigenous communities, suffer a disproportionately high impact from the pollution. Many of the processes I am describing are done at a scale that is almost unimaginable.

With the paper pulp made, and left unbleached, it has to be made into sheets. The thick slurry of fibers suspended in water is floated onto a screen. Below this a bank of hydrofoils whirr away, removing water until the thin sheets are passed over suction boxes that finish removing the water from the sheet.[32] This is a process inherited from hand papermaking where a craftsperson dips a screen in a vat of pulp, shakes it into a thin layer, and presses it flat to remove the water before laying it out to dry. In this industrial version, the pulp drops to the screen and becomes a soft sheet in less than a minute. Then, slippery thin, it passes between rollers that squeeze and compress the fibers. The water is about half gone, so then the continuous stream of paper slides through drying cylinders. Sizing is added, a thin layer of starch that helps the fibers bond inside the paper. Soft, unbleached, and brown with a grainy texture, the paper for the coffee filters is ready to ship in rolls to the next factory site where it will be cut, crimped, and packaged.

The quality control supervisor in the paper factory

sits at a computer watching feeds from various camera eyes and has access to each section of the process. Alarm lights and other warning signs flash if something malfunctions. The steady gaze of the person in the chair does not waver from the screen. They survey every point from the huge vats of pulp through the final inspections to check the dimensions of the sheets and be sure they fall within acceptable ranges of variation. Once the inspection is passed, the paper is rolled into giant reels more than twenty feet long and weighing over a hundred thousand pounds. In other words, these could be lethal if they get loose and run over someone or something in its path. A crane is required to lift the reels to a winder, where it the paper is unrolled and cut for custom purposes, packaged, shipped, and put to use. Each of these stages requires energy, of course, and while many of the steps are automated, human labor is still involved on the factory floor, in the truck driver's cab, in the processes of loading and unloading.

We can pause here a moment and reflect on the scale of the paper industry. More than three hundred million tons of paper are produced in the world in the course of a year.[33] Consider that forty percent of trash waste is composed of paper. The estimate is that every ton of paper uses up more than two-hundred and fifty gallons of gasoline. And paper dust, generated in the production processes of cutting and completing the filters, has an adverse effect on workers' health—sometimes causing conditions as acute as workplace asthma or chronic bronchitis. More affluvia.

The box (heavy paperboard, also a wood product) of coffee filters is replete with statements proclaiming the virtues of these organic and unbleached paper cones. The inks used on this package are all in the earth-toned browns and greens. They provide thumbnail bits of information about the source of materials, composting, disposal, and even instructions on how to open the filter to put it into the cone. The details of manufacture are boasted all over the whole brown box. Recognition of the consumer's superior judgment in picking this particular filter over others is evident.

When my coffee is finished, I remove the used filter, taking a certain satisfaction in the dripping waste that oozes from the bottom and even through the sides. The process of the filter's biodegradable deterioration has begun, but only slowly. Remarkably, the crimped seam still holds even as the bulky weight of the soaked grounds swells the soft wet paper. An unexpected amount of sensuality attaches to this object, as surely as the smooth pressure of the lid of the grinder responding to the palm of my hand returns a tactile pleasure. Similarly, the pop of the cat food can as I pull back on the aluminum tab and the shush of the spoon dipping into the foam of the paté provide their own immediate satisfactions beyond whatever pleasure is afforded to the animals once their bowls are on the floor. The combination of simplicity, direct action, and reassuring repetition of routine never fails. The infrastructure remains intact. I have felt no existential threat in the daily activity until I paused to consider its complexity and my complicity in these larger systems.

The coffee grounds go into my organic garbage, but not a separate compost bin. The downstream life of these materials is another story to be left for another time. The massive flow of garbage and household trash through the processing systems of the City of Los Angeles involves complex engineering of recycling, recovery, what is known as waste-to-energy, and of course landfills. My coffee grounds, possibly begun as a crop of cherries on a mountain in Central America or the plains of Brazil, will find their resting place as organic matter in a site managed by one of the largest cities in America, mixed at random with other trash or biomass, cheek by jowl with who knows what food container, old shoes, or cast-off sponges and household waste mouldering into a material ooze, hotbeds of contaminants and toxins. Los Angeles has recently instituted mandates for composting organic waste, but the scale of the supply stream remains overwhelming.

● ●

Glass Jar for the Beans: Chipped but loyal
I store my coffee beans in a squat, square, glass jar I have owned so long I forget when it came into my life. The cool solid container is almost too big for me to hold in

one hand. I take it carefully from the refrigerator shelf so as not to cut my fingers on the sharply chipped corner caused by an accidental slip some years back. The chip is raw with layered edges, as if the break had revealed sedimentary fault lines. The jar is exactly the right size for a week's beans and I keep it in spite of the risk posed by its dangerous corner. The glass, thick as the goggle lenses, blurs the beans just slightly. The aluminum lid is fitted perfectly to the plastic cuff on the rim, designed to keep moisture out and "the freshness in," as the product's marketers would say. The cuff's translucent white plastic has remained resilient and pliable for many years and the fitted aluminum lid slides off with a satisfying slight "shush" as it separates from the jar. An odd pleasure attaches to the act of pulling it free and shaking the shiny beans into the grinder. The collar makes a perfect barrier between the aluminum lid, with its rounded corners and lightly brushed sheen, and the jar. An ordinary object, as one might use for the storage of beans, rice, or grains since glass jars are ubiquitous.

Glass: Sand to Bottle

Glass occurs in nature, that is, can be formed without human intervention. A lightning strike on sand will make glass naturally by melting. The earliest human experience of the glass may have been hard shiny lumps created by these accidents—some of which can leave pieces of considerable size and dramatic shape behind. A lightning strike passing under a house on sand can leave a jagged zig-zagging form the length of a field. But these actions are unpredictable and not able to be controlled. So we figured out how to make glass for beads, cups, and other objects back in Mesopotamia and Egypt about four thousand years ago.

As already noted, silica is the chief ingredient in glass, much of it from sand. Currently, along with gravel and other soil aggregates, sand is the most mined substance in the world. After water, it is the most consumed by volume.[34] Sand for glass comes from sedimentary deposits of riverbeds and banks—and is composed of tiny bits that are granular and sharp-edged. To my surprise, desert sand is quite different because it is produced by erosion, carried by wind, and not good for glass because of its chemical composition and coarser texture.[35] But beach sand is in such high demand that it is being mined more quickly than it can be replenished. Though hard to imagine given the scale of removal and the amount of conspicuous equipment involved, this leads to unregulated and illegal mining by sand mafias. Even legal mining results in the removal of massive amounts of sand that lowers the riverbeds and causes dramatic changes in ecological systems, leading to increased threat of flooding and other disturbances to landscapes made fragile and unstable. The impact on wildlife is disastrous. Turtle nesting sites and crocodile habitats are reliant on sand banks for hatching their eggs or other survival activities. Indian fish-eating crocodiles, called *ghurials*, have become nearly extinct as the banks of their river environments are removed

Part One: Making Coffee 145

or erode. Aquatic wildlife suffer as the water is disturbed, becoming turbid, impenetrable to sunlight, its oxygen supply damaged. The list of disastrous effects of sand removal goes on, with flooding and erosion at scales that shift the shape of the land and course of water flows.

Sand mining, like many apparently mechanical processes, is also an art. At the Chicago World's Columbian Exposition in 1893 a prize was awarded to a man named Henry Harrison Hunter for the quality of sand he mined in Morgan County, West Virginia. A blue ribbon was awarded in recognition of Hunter's ability to distinguish the best grains. Those days of individual miners are long gone.

Considerable sand mining is done along the shores of Lake Michigan. Dune sand has extraordinary uniformity of size and chemical purity to recommend it. But while Michigan is a major source of sand for molding and casting, California leads the nation in sand for glass production.[36]

Most sand goes into concrete for construction, but glass production relies on either silica or quartz. Grain sizes must meet particular specifications and glass sand must be more than 98% silica. The presence of any metallic oxides will add color to the glass and are considered impurities. The clear, transparent glass we use in casual abundance is the outcome of melting silica and transforming it with intense heat.

146 AFFLUVIA

Diagram 8: The glass jar
Beach sand is collected and shipped to processing plants where it may be mixed with quartz crystals mined and pulverized into fine grains. The sand and silica are mixed with other substances like soda ash and funneled into a furnace heated to about 1550 degrees Celsius (2800 degrees Fahrenheit). The stream of liquid gas is chunked into "gobs" and sent through forming machines to become shapes.

Sand mining is very direct. It consists of equipment that digs the material from the surface—or dredges it from shallow waters–then piles it into open containers or flatbed barges for shipping. The sheer weight and cost of transport makes it most efficient to carry the sand a short distance to a facility where it is pulverized and cleaned. As in so many industrial processes, water is a resource consumed almost without thought, used as a part of the treatment without regard for cost. From the sandstone quarry, the raw material is sent along a conveyor, mixed with water, and put onto a vibrating screen. Slime waste and overflow are pumped out and then the substance is sent through a series of devices with poetic and suggestive names like "attrition scrubber" and a "flotation machine" that removes the "froth impurity" until finally the clean silica is sent for drying, grinding, and to market.[37] The processes are intensely physical—moving, crushing, washing, sorting, vibrating and pouring—and so the equipment is rugged, made with bright enamel-coated surfaces and strong steel frames.

The tank trucks of clean silica arrive at the glass factory and empty their loads through hoses and pipes that funnel down into a furnace. Along with the clean dry sand, a mass of recycled glass called "cullet" is also part of the mix. Cullet shines brilliantly as light strikes each facet of the pulverized grains. The effect is particularly striking when the mass is in motion, a living stream of refraction and reflection. This recycled glass is no longer a natural substance and follows its own supply chain and lifecycle from collection and washing, sorting, purifying and crushing, before it is sold and shipped. Recycled glass has to be sorted by color, either at the collection point, or further along in the process. Optical scanners can automatically sort by color in at reprocessing plants, aiding the process particularly for high volumes of materials. Glass is characterized as "infinitely recyclable" because it can be made back into cullet time after time, melted, shaped, and put back into circulation as bottles or jars—or used in construction materials—though not without costs of all kinds.

To summarize so far, the manufacture of my glass jar may have involved a massive excavation on the edges of Lake Michigan, shipping and sorting, and arrival at a factory where these materials meet the recycled cullet harvested from milk bottles, jelly jars, pickle and mustard containers or any of an enormous number of other clear glass vessels now pulverized so that they blend into a single stream of usable sharp-edged glittering grains.

Now I find out about the other ingredients involved in the manufacture of glass. For sheet and bottle glass, soda ash (sodium carbonate) is used to reduce the melting point of silica. This in turn decreases the amount of energy required for the enormous furnaces in which the mixture of sand and cullet becomes liquid. Soda ash is also produced through extraction, mining, processing. The raw material is crushed, mixed with water, heated, filtered, turned into a highly saturated solution from which the water is evaporated to leave crystals that are "dewatered" in centrifuges and finally fed to rotary kilns as finished soda ash ready for shipping and transport.

Limestone is another additive, used to reduce viscosity and make glass easier to handle. In technical terms, the limestone is said to improve the "melting kinetics," but this behavior depends upon having homogeneously sized limestone particles, a specific chemical composition suited to use in container glass, and a supply chain capable of meeting demand. Controlling dust and moisture along the production process of the limestone is key. Once again we are in a physical world of manufacture, with grinding, crushing, washing and drying all essential to creating a refined product that is a key part of another industry. Like turtles all the way down, industrial processes spiral into a network of codependent manufacturing details, each a specialized industry with its own expertise, outputs—and affluvia.

In our story, we now arrive at the glass factory where a huge tank truck empties its load of purified silica into hoses and pipes. Fittings and hardware, pumps and pressure systems, a whole interconnected system coordinates the transfer. The silica gets mixed with the cullet, soda ash, and limestone. The sound of dry ingredients running through pipes and funnels is like a waterfall of beads running in the background. Everything skitters across metal surfaces and through down chutes in an efficient low-friction stream.[38]

Once all ingredients are mixed, the batch is funneled into the furnace. The mixture becomes liquid when heated by gas and electricity to about 1550 Celsius (about 2800 Fahrenheit). This is about the same temperature required for iron to melt (by contrast, lead melts at 327 Celsius, gold at 1063, steel 1350-1460). The technology for making glass was, like that of working metal, dependent on developing the ability to make hot enough fires. Even in their earliest versions the furnaces produced greenhouse gases in the form of carbon monoxide, carbon dioxide, and various other emissions. But now, many glass furnaces are never turned off, producing a steady stream of emissions. The workers tending the furnace wear hard hats and goggles and stare into the blaring interior through porthole openings. They hold dark film in front of their eyes to mask the glare.

If we follow the process, then we see the white-hot molten liquid stream out into a cooling area, called the refiner, where it sits in large basins. Over their openings a large barrier crown of non-flammable material keeps the molten glass contained while also letting air circulate. Gas trapped in the glass during the manufacturing process escapes into the air. Still molten, the glass flows into a fore-hearth, an area where it continues to cool to a uniform temperature. Heat is expelled at every step. Then the stream of liquid glass, pouring like a thick ribbon from the machine, is cut into "gobs" still glowing white hot. These liquid pucks of molten glass are shot through "gravity slides" into forming machines where compressed air is used to force the liquid glass into specific shapes. These molds create the negative interior space of the container whether it is a bottle, glass, or jar. While all of this is about what I would expect, the heat, glare, and management of molten glass still feels daunting.

While the bottles or jars are still hot, they pass through a coating hood where they are treated with another chemical substance, monobutyltinchloride (MBTC), applied in the form of a vapor. The MBTC oxidizes on the surface of the glass objects and this helps keeps them from scratching. MBTC is one of a large family of "organotin" compounds, most of which are classified as eye and skin irritants. If swallowed, ingredients in the compound can induce various symptoms such as nausea, vomiting, and more severe side-effects. But in the glass factory, the yellowish oily substance is not particularly volatile. The bottles and jars then pass through another heating and cooling process known as annealing, which helps equalize the strength of the glass throughout. A final coating of polyurethane is applied that also helps protect against breakage and abrasion. Polyurethane? A polymer compound first manufactured in Germany in the 1930s by Otto Bayer, then taken up at grand scale in the 1950s by Dow, DuPont, Union Carbide, and Monsanto, giants in the chemical industries. These coatings also provide some protection against ultra-violet radiation, adding some longevity to products in the glass storage. These two steps have brought workers into contact with highly toxic substances that release vapors into the air. More affluvia.

The glass factory is a fretwork of steel, platforms, pipes and machinery all designed to move these different components through stages of the process. These are assembly line processes, not artisanal glass blowing and craft operations. The spaces are industrial, large hangars and enclosed atriums with open spans allow maximum circulation of air and light. The workers tending the machines wear asbestos gloves and suits and carefully tend the conveyor belts and ovens, fully aware of the heat and the interlocking systems through which the molten substance moves until it leaves the factory as bottles and jars.

The cuff: Familiar plastic
As to the plastic cuff on my jar, the it is either PVC or acrylic, the former is made mainly of salt and oil, the latter of polymers chemically produced like the other plastics for the gas valve and grinder lid, both already described. Ultimately, whether made in a lab or from mined materials, these substances depend on

extraction industries. We are always, constantly, taking material from the earth and transforming it through various processes at an enormous scale.

The shiny lid: Another metal
The form-fitting aluminum lid made of brushed aluminum has, of course, its own history of manufacture. Though aluminum is a common metal, it doesn't appear as an independent substance in nature (unlike gold, silver, or copper). Aluminum has to be smelted—heated to separate it from other materials—in a process that requires so much electricity that the plants are usually located near a hydroelectric plant.

Once again, we begin with the raw material, in this case an aluminum-rich ore, bauxite. The full lifecycle begins with mining (extraction again), then processing, and finally an electrolytic reduction using electricity. Clear as can be. Hardly. A sedimentary rock with many minerals in it, in its raw form, bauxite looks like cement full of caramelized pebbles. It is found in many places in the world, but is in large supply in Australia, China, Guinea, Brazil, and Jamaica. Enormous reserves have been located in Viet Nam, though not mined extensively.[39] Strip mining and open pit mines are common, but deeper mines are also dug to reach reserves below the surface. By now, these processes of excavation, repeated across the stories of lifecycles of materials, are familiar, but that does not reduce their impact.

Diagram 9: Aluminum

Bauxite miners cut through many layers of rocky earth, sometimes using explosives to loosen the ore, which is then washed repeatedly in a processing plant, releasing many waste products and fumes, including some that are radioactive. Tailings produced by the aluminum plant seep into streams and water supplies while the factory releases carbon dioxide and heat into the air. The aluminum is heated to a liquid state and then turned into wire, rods, and sheets and cooled.

Part One: Making Coffee 155

In their public relations literature, the mining companies cite special equipment used to cut through layer after layer of rock being transported. But the language of the mining industry rarely speaks of human labor, workers, conditions, or costs. Is it hot work? Does dust pollute the air? Are there waste products being washed away, into water streams or onto nearby land? What does the light look like shining from these surfaces and reflecting from the metal structures of the factories? In photographs, huge areas of red mud appear as part of the bauxite production process—wet fields of a thick red-brown paste full of silicon, irons, titanium and other compounds. The fields are left to evaporate and percolate, with many of their components able to be reclaimed and used. Meanwhile, the bauxite becomes a bright white powder. Who witnesses this? Who has the knowledge to know when each stage of the process is complete and the substances can be moved to the next step? Who regulates the industry?

I find it fascinating to think about the historical changes brought about as chemical industries escalated to mass scale. Many physical and chemical discoveries are associated with individual scientists who invented them, so that the names Hall-Héroult process or Deville process connect contemporary activity to a long history of laboratory experiments. For instance, the Bayer process by which bauxite is turned into aluminum was invented a century ago. This built on 19th century extraction and processing, but involved vehicles, equipment, objects, and manufacture that had not been part of the earlier phase of industrialization. The early 20th century witnessed a major escalation in chemical processing. No precedent for such large scale or transformative processes existed before the early 20th century and the interdependencies that have developed in the supply chains are now what makes them both robust and fragile.

The Bayer Process is used by 80% of aluminum plants in the world. The language used in the industrial description for the processes is vivid: the original ore, mixed with lye and caustic soda (eats your flesh) is subject to what is known as "grinding and digestion"—the equivalent of your stomach if it were a combination of pulverizing machine and cement mixer. Yummy. This initial process spits out "spent liquor" (which is a long way from whiskey), and "digestion discharge" (which is all too easily imagined). Then a series of washings, with sand, are followed by separation. Through filtration, the "pregnant liquor" is shunted off to be further subjected to processes that result in the precipitation of the hydrated alumina. A calcination process turns out the final product, and along the way, waste water is produced at every stage. Waste is a generic term. It simply signals something thrown away, not able to be used, marketed, turned into products. The realities are far more toxic. The generic term TENORM—technologically enhanced naturally occurring radioactive material points to a wide

Part One: Making Coffee

variety of these released substances.

The "tailings" or waste products from the first set of processes of ore into aluminum are disposed of, and for every ton of alumina made from the ore, more than double that weight in waste is generated. The image of these vastly uneven piles rises in my mind's eye, one refined and petite, the other large and sloppy, a combination of rock, mud, and other materials filled with a variety of minerals. A sludgy red mud can dry to a fine powder in solid form that can be processed again to extract aluminum oxide. More water, more energy, more waste. But the red mud is also both caustic (it burns) and radioactive (high risk) and contains elevated levels of arsenic and chromium. So now this toxic sludge is channeled into an "impoundment" lined with clay or some other barrier to seepage. More processes, more energy, more water, more waste. A trail of industrial activity connects this waste to a host of other processes that generate their own problems and contribute pollutants and toxins. In the end, less than 3% of bauxite residuals (a polite term) can be put to any kind of productive use. The smell of it all is overwhelming.

The final stage of aluminum processing involves electrolysis, facilitated by yet another rare mineral, cryolite. Seen from the air, one cryolite mine in Greenland looked like a gravel pit with a small cluster of tiny houses at its edge, as close to the operations as possible. A tanker ship sat in the water nearby, a large crane with a delivery system for the raw material balanced in the air, its counterweight keeping the whole huge arm in place. The idea that all of this—extraction, mining, shipping, processing, enormous equipment, planning, infrastructure—was required just to create cryolite as part of a single phase of a complex process is hard to grasp. An entire community was organized around this single spot of earth. A group of workers, no doubt well-known to each other, small as the housing cluster appears to be, toiled in the Greenland climate to keep a stream of this mineral moving into the supply chain. Now the site is closed. Cryolite is being manufactured artificially–which simply means other materials are extracted and transformed. The language of smelting and sintering of the many minerals and chemicals speaks to the highly developed level of specialized expertise in the production of aluminum and other metals.[40]

I feel compelled to finish the lifecycle story of cryolite and electrolysis, though I am awash in chemical and industrial processes and have nearly forgotten how they interconnect. The electrolytic reduction takes place in a separate space where large open buildings containing up to hundreds of "reduction cells" are connected to electrical power sources that run a constant current through them. The voltage required to run the process is a thousand times greater than what is needed to start a car engine. This massive amount of electricity creates a conductive environment in highly controlled circumstances. The current breaks a bond between the aluminum and oxygen in the molten cryolite. The aluminum settles out while the oxygen bonds with carbon to make carbon dioxide. The aluminum is extracted from the cells with a vacuum bucket by way of a hole punched in the cryolite crust that has formed. Got that? More pipes, more specialized equipment, more power and more toxic gases released. Imagine being tasked with designing these procedures.

The liquid aluminum is taken to a cast house, turned into ingots that can be re-melted and made into any specified form. Where, how, by whose hands and labor are the ingots packed, shipped, transported then unpacked, melted, and cast in molds designed for specific purposes? The physical structures of these factory spaces are almost generic in appearance, constructed from steel platforms and scaffolding. The concrete floors shine with reflected light from the bright bulbs suspended in the ceiling while palettes sit stacked and ready for a forklift as the ongoing pounding, driving, pulsating rhythms of the reduction or casting or waste processing take place. How many such factories in how many parts of the world are required to meet the demands for aluminum?

I push the lid of the glass canister back into place, its rounded corners slipping easily into position. Nothing in my gesture or the feel and appearance of the object offers any evidence of this story of production. All of it is concealed from view through habits of use.

● ●

The Coffee Maker: Miracles of circuitry
The many processes of extraction and industrial production involved in plastic, metal, and paper have their roots in physical and chemical processes that developed across

millennia. True, the production of synthetic materials was largely a 20th century contribution, but in the coffee maker, we encounter those uniquely contemporary inventions—electronic circuits and digital processors. First, attention to another physical feature and then on to the miniature electronic miracles.

Canister: Insulation mysteries

The plastic handle attached to smooth brushed aluminum canister was created through the same process as the hard shell of the coffee grinder. The shiny black plastic collar and lid have multiple design features. A slot allows the dripping coffee to flow through the opening. A little button that presses against the drip spout and its spring lets me interrupt the percolation to pour my coffee. The spring closes the spout, the coffee accumulates in the filter basket, and only a drip or two hits the hot plate on which the canister rests when I pull it free to pour my first cup. Amazing to think how much engineering has gone into these ordinary objects. We already know the story of the lid's plastic and small spring from the grinder.

As just detailed, the aluminum in the pot, like all metals, begins with a gash in the ground and human labor aided by machines that dig, grind, and carry materials away from the site as in the production of the glass jar lid. At these sites, the smell of diesel exhaust hangs in the dust-thickened air. The winds carry the pollutants into nearby villages and towns where it settles on crops in fields, entering the bloodstream through digestion. We have been here before. No need to repeat the story of bauxite mining and electrolytic reduction from the previous section.

But now to the weird insulation. Turns out the canister is a double structure, two cylinders fitted one inside the other. I see only shiny surfaces on the inside and outside. But with a bit of research I find online cutaway views and learn that a gap filled with foam-based insulation exists between the outer and inner forms. This creates a thermal barrier to keep the heat of the coffee inside.

But what kind of foam goes into this cavity? I imagine the kind of sickish-yellow spray foam applied as insulation to walls, blown into the interstices of studs applied by workers in haz-mat suits holding nozzle spray guns in construction sites. But surely that is not how the foam got into my canister. The foam in the coffee canister turns out to a plastic insulation that is very bad at conducting heat. No dancing atoms.

At the high end of coffee devices, the brew is kept warm with an insulating vacuum. Think of the elegant mirrored glass interior of an expensive thermos, for instance, which provides a thermal buffer between the liquid and an airless chamber. Exactly how does this work? I am not quite sure except that in reading further I find that the silver on the glass actually helps reduce infrared radiation which I did not even know was there. This radiation is described as an

Part One: Making Coffee

effect of the vibration caused by atomic motion. Ok, I am willing to believe this, but I don't have a clue as to how that radiation is generated by a liquid inside a thermos, unless this is simply another term for heat (thermal radiation). Heat cannot be transferred across a vacuum since it lacks atoms available to participate in transmission of energy.

Somehow I have shifted from an image of swaddling my coffee canister in a warm fuzzy foam to the serious realm of atomic physics. Clearly, a vacuum-based thermos is a finely designed work of human engineering and thermodynamic control. The coffee remains hot.

But my humble canister is a mid-level range appliance, not a high-end designer model. The dull sound made when it is tapped on the outer shell suggests insulation rather than a vacuum and the space between the two fitted cylinders is most likely filled with polyurethane. Nothing eats polyurethane, for better and for worse, and so it is unlikely to be attacked by mold or other micro-organisms. I can't see the plastic insulation, so I can only speculate, and when I search for information, I as usual find a whole new descriptive vocabulary of feature promotion. The foam is described as "closed-cell and cross-linked" and it is usually vacuum-formed to fit. Here we go again, into the rabbit holes of specialized industries.

One insulation company, Zotek, brags about its products "consistently out-performing" others on the market.[41]

Zotek's insulation is made from nylon, and the manufacturing process is described in a recorded webinar introduced by a white male scientist in khakis and a blue shirt, microphone neatly clipped to the inside of his collar, who stands in a brightly lit industrial space. Behind him, ductwork, steel fretwork, cars with wheels stacked with freshly minted slabs of insulation are all visible in the pristine space. See, this is a good clean industry producing barely any dust. In addition to insulating my coffee, keeping it warm-ish during the first hours of the morning, the foam has a role to play in aviation, automotive, and other engineering sectors of manufacture. The scientist stands tall.

The production process begins with delivery of polymer granules into outdoor silos whose bright clean metallic surfaces shine. These repositories hold the bead-like granules until they are fed through a chute into a hopper and mixed with additives. The granules are mostly made from recycled plastics, and at present the largest supplier in the global market is Indian Polymers. The photograph of their factory shows a phantasmagorical scene with many towers, pipes, ramps, open staircases, and infrastructure elements shining under lights against the night sky like some incredible installation on Mars or the moon, pounding, clanging, hissing away with its pistons, valves, and gears. The output results in a wide array of brightly colored pellets, each pristine and attractive looking, ready for use in every conceivable synthetic color of the polymer rainbow. But now these pellets must be turned into a foamy substance. The giant, specialized equipment in the factory consists of conveyors and gears, chambers that are sealed so that an "extrusion" process transforms polymer granules into slabs of newly formed material. The story of production is a smooth one, constant motion through multiple phases. Rollers move the continuous slab along a belt from the oven, through a cutting mechanism, from which the flat units of material fall into a neat stack. The solid sheets of polymer are black, shiny, and flexible, about the size of a bathmat. In the next stage they are put into a high-pressure autoclave, heated above melting point, and saturated with nitrogen. Heat, pressure, and then cooling result in the absorption of nitrogen. These slabs are again heated under moderate pressure, and in this phase, the nitrogen expands and turns the slab into a larger sheet. Starting from bathmat size, the final sheet is larger than a hollow-core door, light, flexible, and spongy—filled with gas bubbles. Making sense? Every detail raises questions. How is something "saturated with nitrogen" and what is the source of the gas? The description only makes me aware of my ignorance.

Talcum powder, a release agent used to spring the sheets loose, is then rinsed off before they are stacked and wrapped in plastic sheeting for shipping. While talc is a naturally-occurring mineral that is highly moisture absorbent, it also contains traces of asbestos which are harmful to humans. Talc mines of considerable scale exist in Luzenac, France, and in Western Australia, though the name derives from an ancient Persian word. The talc mining operation in France has the spectacular beauty of a series of ancient ziggurats, its stepped platforms linked by broad flat roadways all stark white against the rural green countryside and dramatic mountains. This particular mining operation is essential to obtain a powder that will be used so that the polymer sheets that will become insulation pop easily out of their molds. One small step in a long series of operations.

Heat and electricity are absorbed in each stage of polymer production, and every piece of the large equipment has dozens of heavy-duty wires, plugs, fans, and exhaust valves. The autoclaves are precision-engineered pieces of specialized equipment whose ability to produce pressure and hold heat is crucial. Hoses and fittings, smoothly operating wheels and tight-sealing steel chambers are essential. Once the materials are slid into the autoclave and sealed, the control of the process is done through computer programs that closely monitor the elimination of oxygen from the chambers. Programmers, systems engineers, designers—the range of skilled workers involved is staggering.

The language of the industry information stresses that the insulating material has many positive characteristics. It is lightweight, resistant, self-sealing, ultra-pure, and has remarkable impact strength. No doubt. But the spokespeople describe their product as if it were fully autonomous, had no connection to human work or effort. The properties of the material and even the processes are a point of pride, and neither the product nor its lifecycle are connected to ecological or social systems in the description. The entire description is without any pause or hesitation, as if it all took place seamlessly in a clean machine world where everything works perfectly.

All this just to create the material to insulate my coffee pot... I have not described how the insulation gets between the two walls of the canister, but we are moving on, figuring that it is surely blown in under pressure.

A couple of features on the coffee maker involve technologies we have not yet examined—LEDs, LCDs, electronic circuits, and digital components. Now we are in high tech zones.

LEDs: Excitation of electrons
I stare at the glowing blue LED lights around the buttons on my brewing device, noting their sinister air. Glowing blue in the early morning dark, they seem unflinching, soulless, and inorganic in a way that feels threatening. In fact, the "light" they exude is different from that of traditional lights. Think of Thomas Edison and his bulbs—a filament of wire gets an electrical charge that excites electrons momentarily

until they drop back in disappointment and photons are discharged, radiating soft illumination and heat.

LED lights also glow from excitation of electrons. But they do not give off heat. They are cold light, which is perhaps why they feel sinister. LED means light-emitting-diode. "Light-emitting" is clear, but what is a "diode"? Some details: A diode is a two-layer semi-conductor in which one layer has an excess of electrons and the other has a shortfall. Imagine if the energy if one side of a subway car were too full and the other too empty and the passengers got into an altercation and began to switch sides. To increase the activity in this diode system, certain impurities are entered in the manufacturing process. Again, by analogy, think about a bad odor on one side of that subway and an annoyingly hot blast of heat on the other. These negative effects would amplify the crowd's interest in moving around. Better yet, just pass around a bunch of beers, joints, and cocktails, and see how the crowd interaction changes. That's the state of excited electrons. They like to party freely with other atoms.

In LEDs the impurities that get added are zinc and nitrogen. The result is a material developed at Stanford in the early 1970s, "zinc-doped gallium nitride" which I will not even try to understand except that it definitely sounds just like something made in

Part One: Making Coffee

California in the 70s... Instead of the diodes being enclosed in glass, the light emitting system is encased in our favorite material, plastic, which supposedly makes it durable. So, the over-excited material is sealed in plastic in a condition of frustration that keeps its electron transfer trapped to produce light.

Creating the LED semiconductor "wafer" is a high tech esoteric process. Unlike Edison's lightbulb, which, conceivably, could be replicated at home with a bit of tungsten, a sealed glass jar, and a current, a semiconductor can only be produced in high pressure and high temperature "clean" conditions. In the industry, they speak of "growing" the wafers from a mix of such things as the gallium mentioned above, arsenic, and phosphor each purified and mixed into a highly concentrated solution. Gallium? A soft silvery metal, present in the periodic table, discovered by a Frenchman in the 19th century. Though it doesn't occur "freely" in nature, it is closely connected with bauxite in aluminum, it is mainly used as an alloy to alter the properties of other metals. In the semiconductor it aids somehow in creating violet and blue light from diodes to brighten the LED display in my kitchen.

Now to the arsenic. Oh, right. This occurs in all manner of foods, shellfish and other fish, is present in the earth's crust, has its source in volcanic action, and is also used in metal alloys for the properties it lends to the materials. In the Bronze age, it was used to make metal harder. Toxic, to be sure, when ingested directly, in food substances, from contaminated ground water, and from the air. As the Wiki will tell you, it was referred to as the "poison of kings" for its popularity as a substance used to eliminate enemies or uncooperative family members. Curiously, absorbed in small doses over time, it produces immunity protecting those women who ate it mixed with chalk as a way to make their skin pale. Compared with the carefully terraced bauxite mines, the sites of arsenic removal look rough and craggy, and over time the arsenic produces encrustations on the surfaces of the exposed rocks in the quarries. Research shows that the greatest number of people at risk near arsenic mining sites are in Bangladesh, West Bengal, and the Chaco-Pampean Plain in Argentina.[42]

In addition to the arsenic, zinc, nitrogen, and gallium, the LEDs contain phosphor. Phosphor. The very name seems mythical, as if the luminescence were the work of some animate spirit. Indeed, the substance glows when exposed to radiant energy. Who wouldn't? Their outer electrons get excited, and as they cool back down, they release the energy as light just like the tungsten filaments in Edison's bulbs. This is a deeply poetic image, a cycle of excitation and release, the afterglow of exposure. The process is technically known as scintillation. The language of chemistry is highly suggestive. Incoming particles excite electrons, but there are "impurities" that create energy levels in a "forbidden gap" in the structure of the crystal lattice. Electrons get "captured" by "impurity centers" and "de-excitation" is slowed by a "low-probability forbidden mechanism" all of which amounts to saying, again, that after the energy rises, it falls, and is released as light.[43] The details of the chemical processes are endlessly interesting, but they also produce a very long trail of research, deeper and deeper into information about wavelength emissions of different structures and their color temperatures and decay times.

The blue of the LED is a color not seen in the natural world, its "electroluminescence" is "exploited" for backlight and nightlight displays. The history of phosphor in technologies of light displays includes all kinds of familiar and now vanished objects from cathode-ray-tubes in old televisions, those bulky-bodied monsters of my childhood with their slow-fading light, to oscilloscopes, with their green lines glowing on a dark background. The phosphor on these screens was deposited as a powder, or on a film behind the glass, so that the signals could be made visible through carefully directed excitation.

The buttons continue to glow at me in the still dark kitchen. They are a reminder that this is an electronic appliance, part of the new world now and not merely some mechanical instrument.

Digital Clock: Backlight and crystal
Every single one of these minor-seeming components of my coffee maker turns out to be crazy complicated. The LCD clock, for instance, is made of a "real-time clock circuit" and a liquid crystal display, illumination source, backlight control circuit, power supply, and master control unit. What? All that so I can see the time in digits? What is a "liquid crystal" and how does it produce light?

When I find the patent information on this device, I see it contains a description of the ways the "indicating elements" are combined to make the characters or numbers whose positions indicate the time.[44] The amount of engineering involved—and that has evolved—in this tiny detail allows the light-emitting intensity to be varied, controlled in what feels like real time. The notion of "real-time" is too complex to unravel, depending as it does on human perception on a rotating earth and other factors that turn a relative metric into the illusion of a transcendent one. But that is a story for another time, pun intended, and so let's just stick to understanding how the LCD works.

I learn a lot from the community of Ham Radio people, who generously share their knowledge of

Part One: Making Coffee 173

Diagram 10: LCD, Liquid crystal display

The LCD sandwich consists of many layers. The backlight unit contains a bottom chassis, reflector sheet, light guide plate, LED strip, diffuser sheet, prism sheet, and bottom polarizer. The LCD panel has a bottom glass, a thin film transistor, a layer of liquid crystal, a common electrode, an RGB (red/green/blue) color filter, and a top glass. These are covered by the top polarizer and top chassis. The materials that go into producing these layers include chemicals, plastics, metals, glass, gold, iron, copper, quartz and of course heat and energy for production.

this technology.[45] They reveal that the LCD is a "sandwich" in which a liquid crystalline substance is squeezed between polarizing filters with a light source behind this arrangement. By selectively filtering the light, the polarizing filters turn an area bright or dark. The secret to this is a collection of long "twisted crystals" in the sandwich layer which are kept from following their impulse to rotate. This sounds unkind, but such rotation would bring them into alignment with the polarization, ruining the effects. The crystalline structure is organized into patterns such as segments or pixels which can be activated selectively with electrical voltage. As the voltage is turned on, the twisted crystals align. We are back to microscopic levels of excitement producing macroscopic effects. The great advantage of LCDs over earlier technology, those CRTs (cathode ray tubes) of yore, is that they consume less energy and dissipate much less as well. However, the LCDs are actually more complicated, made of up to fourteen layers of different thin films, each with different capacities. Each has its own production process and lifecycle.

I glean more details from the site of the wonderfully erudite nerds of "Circuits Today" who explain that the "liquid crystal" combines solid and liquid states in its basic physical condition, hence its name. Unlike LEDs, described above, the liquid crystal requires a light source and does not generate light itself. The layers of material go into making a standard LCD include a frame, cover glass, polarizing film, a glass filter, character generating layer, the liquid crystal and then more glass, polarizing film, and a mirrored surface, among others. For the glass, we are back in the world of silicon and sand. For film in the realm of plastics. And for the liquid crystal? The material was invented, accidentally, in the late 1880s by a botanist named Friedrich Reinitzer who was playing around with a substance extracted from, of all things, carrots. The name for the substance came from a German physicist, Otto Lehman, who published a piece titled "Flüssige Kristalle" (literally "liquid crystal") in 1904. Other inventors and scientists played around with the substance, but industrial applications and uses were not developed until the 1960s when a researcher at RCA Laboratories realized a matrix of the substance would respond to voltage in a way that made it highly useful in visual displays. Now we are getting somewhere. In current technology, LCDs are everywhere—in televisions, cameras, watches, phones, computer monitors and making flat screen displays possible.

The crucial material in LCDs—aside from the glass, film, and polarizing filters—is the liquid crystal itself. As so often in these investigation, I find myself once again plunged into specialized vocabulary that describes industrial processes in which chemical compounds are produced and manipulated. While the details are too technical for me to follow, the basic story is that the molecules in the substance line up in different ways at different phases or states when the crystal is more or less liquid. The molecules have very nice characteristics, it appears, possessed as they are of a "rigid backbone" and "easily polarizable" aspects.[47] The basic elements are carbon, nitrogen, hydrogen, and oxygen—common in organic compounds—and as crystals, their microscopic structure is highly organized. All of this structure is able to be produced in the lab—or, as many YouTube videos will tell you, at home. Remember those carrots.

But large-scale manufacture of LCDs involves specific kinds of glass, various electronic components that are integrated circuits, and a power supply along with a mechanical frame to hold everything together. The process involves many individual procedures at a micro-level. The glass, for instance, cannot contain certain kinds of ions or they will wander to its surface, combine with moisture, and mess up the electric field pattern. Bad ions. In other words, at the micro level of molecular activity, the glass must be kept from interfering in the way the liquid crystal sandwiched in its small panes behaves. Coating the glass is one solution, but using plastic is another.

All of these components must be cut and some have to be polished. The cutting is done with diamond saw, and this has its own long manufacturing history. The equipment just for producing this one step of the process is also purpose-specific with multiple steps in its process, not to mention sourced materials with their own extraction industries and labor costs, transportation, pollution, and off-gassing. One layer is printed with an electrode pattern made of yet another complex substance—indium tin oxide—applied either by photolithography or silkscreen.[48] Right. These printing techniques in turn have their own sets of equipment for creating and transferring images by using plates, screens, roller, squeegees, inks, stencils, photography or digital imaging. On top of these patterns come coatings of various polymers, some of which are designed to control the way the molecules in the liquid

Part One: Making Coffee 177

crystal line up. Sealing resin and plastic spacers to keep the glass separated properly are sometimes supplemented with plastic beads of uniform size placed in the liquid crystal itself. Polarizing film adds legibility and once this sandwich is assembled, and the liquid crystal fills the space between the two tiny sheets of glass or plastic, the whole unit is ready to be connected to the circuit boards.

This discussion barely scratches the surface. A full account for this one element of the coffee maker, this insignificant LCD clock inserted in its face, a minor bit of its overall machinery, would take pages and pages of elaborate description of sourced materials, manufacturing processes, and engineering feats. The sheer amount of industrial research involved in understanding how different materials behave and what their capacity is for any specific purpose would no doubt have baffled the original botanist gazing with wonder at the activities of his carrot-derived compound. In how many labs and factories, in how many cities and countries, are researchers testing compounds daily to see what else can be conjured from this alchemy of science and invention?

One more small detail to consider in relation to LCDs is the digital font, which has a unique history. While Microsoft cites a 1990s design created by Alan Birch, calling it futuristic and high-tech looking, FontSpace suggested a different origin for the 7-part character that is standard for the font.[49] The character sets by Sizenko Alexander from 2008 contains, for instance, "104 code-points in 76 glyphs." That phrase points to a whole system of standards for font display and design in the production of letterforms within digital and electronic domains. Who learns these codes of design and where are they taught? What apprenticeship does someone like Sizenko Alexander follow to be able to create a character that conforms to those requirements? MIT? Carnegie Mellon? Other schools that combine technical and design curricula?

But pausing, here, and making a careful examination of the font reveals considerable sophistication in the details. A comparison of curves and joints in the forms of the numerals shows fine-tuned and varied attention to joins and abutments of the lines. The numbers are not fully symmetrical or predictable in their shapes, but they share enough characteristics to create stylistic identity. As with everything in this entire process of analysis, what appears simple, turns out to be incredibly complex.[50] All of this disappears in the glow of the LCD in the morning kitchen.

Perhaps the most significant feature of the clock has yet to be mentioned. It is connected to a programmable circuit in an electronic system that links the copper heating element, the thermostat feedback mechanism, a fuse, heater, and transformer as well as the hotplate under the canister, and, of course, programs a beeping tone to signal when the coffee is brewed. I never program the machine, never use its automatic settings to let it know to start my coffee before I wake, partly because I suspect that fresh ground beans would dry out overnight and not provide the same rich taste. A self-cleaning option I have also never used contains a sensor that communicates with the water reservoir. Their exchange is designed to alert me to buildups of calcification, but somehow the message has never reached me. Human-machine communication still has a way to go.

Digitl circuits: Computers on my counter
But let's come back to the fundamental point: my coffee maker is programmable. This single detail is, again, so familiar that we hardly question it punching in times and setting the machine to make coffee at a particular moment. Though I don't use this feature, it is there, another marvel of 21st century engineering considered so trivial that it simply comes as a standard feature of my machine.

With a bit of internet searching, I find out the basics, though I do not really understand what I am reading. For instance, the programmable timer circuit is made of a "14-stage binary counter."[51] Input gates. Truth tables. Programmable switches. I have no idea what these are, only that they are the way the formal logic of decision making essential to circuits is encoded in the physical hardware of the circuit board.

As the basis of all electronics, the circuit board is a quintessentially modern, even contemporary, object. Try looking up the description of this ubiquitous item. The fundamentals indicate that this "semiconductor wafer" has thousands, even millions, of electrical elements on it. These go by the names of resistors, capacitors, diodes, and transistors—each of which manages the flow of current slightly differently. A resistor limits flow. A capacitor stores energy. A diode has two poles. A transistor controls current. What does all of that mean?

Electricity, to be looked at later in its own lifecycle of generation to use in the kitchen appliances, involves the flow of electrical charge. When electricity moves through a circuit it is channeled through pathways that have a logical structure to them controlled by Boolean algebra conceived by George Boole, a 19th century mathematician. Boole defined the logic of decision-making protocols in their most basic form: *and*, *or*, and *not* (referred to more technically as conjunction, disjunction, and negation). From this simple set of elements a complex set of patterns of decision making can be made to control the flow of current or signals. Boole's accomplishments changed the course of history. He provided a system of logic that could be applied to the field of engineering. His poetically titled *Laws of Thought* (1854) has proved controversial in its long-standing suggestion that the human mind is also structured according to these logical systems and can thus be compared with a computer. But Boole's logical primitives undergird the mathematics of information processing across almost all electronic systems of communication, processing, storage, and retrieval (or did until quantum computing developed).

Part One: Making Coffee

Start reading about digital circuits and you are drawn into another mess of linked information. Images of those insect-like chips with their pointed feet and hard silicon bodies appear attached to a board with a labyrinth of metal wiring screen or printed on it. The pattern is deliberate, carefully engineered to create two different kinds of circuits—combinatoric and sequential. Either decisions are being made from a list of possible options and combinations, or they are moving along in a branching sequence of options. This is already more detail than most non-engineers need, and the principle is that these tiny components manage to organize the flow of electrical current in such a way that things get done in the world. Code is transferred. Programs are activated. Levers move, lights flash, heavy equipment is put into place and vast amounts of money are shifted in every instant of every day simply by virtue of having a particular pulse of electricity follow the patterns in the circuit.[52] And of course, the chips are made of silicon. Beach sand. We've been here before, to the mining, extraction, removal of massive amounts of sand because when it is processed it is highly resistant to electrical current. All those little pathways and logical diagrams printed onto it can work without risk—except to the ecological systems from which the resources are extracted. In additions, the production of silicon chips requires ultra-clean rooms, complex specialized equipment, and all the many interdependent systems of mining, processing, transportation and production.

Back to our little clock and the programmable component to which it is attached. The clock must keep constant time if it is to be set to start the coffee maker at a particular moment in the day. Constant time is a fiction. On earth, as human creatures, we use the rotation of the globe and its return to a position in the sky as a way to measure a day. Since we are always moving around the sun, however, that same rotation period is ever so slightly different from what it would be if we measured our day by what is known as sidereal time—when the same celestial objects are visible in the same position in the sky. Aside from this little problem, the issue of computing time in a standard way through an electrical circuit requires that it either include or be connected to some time-keeping device. How does that work? This little digital window on my coffee maker poses its own conundrum.

A clock pulse is like a little electronic heartbeat. The pulse can be generated without any connection to a universal clock or source. An oscillator combined with a series of resistors and capacitors—those tiny elements that either reduce or intensify current—sends an impulse through a circuit of programmable switches. All of this is unimaginably tiny. None of it can be seen with the naked eye, only grasped with the mind's capacity to visualize tightly engineered operations at a micro-scale because all the actual processing happens inside the chips. Beautiful diagrams map the circuitry between labyrinthine pathways and elaborate geometric patterns whose organization makes the elegance of reasoning apparent in diagrammatic form. All of this is part of the innocent seeming clock on my coffee maker.

Part One: Making Coffee

A single pulsing chip, programmed to translate an electrical impulse into a regular metric pattern, can be attached to or coupled with another chip capable of holding an algorithm that in turn can be programmed to turn a device on at a given moment in the sequence of electrical events. The timer does not need to know anything about the rotation of the earth, the human perception of hours and minutes, or have any other reference to the world. It merely needs to know at what point in a particular sequence of highly controlled and discrete logical events it should activate another chain of events. Amazing.

Batteries: Esoteric toxins

The instructions for programming are given by a human operator who merely manipulates the interface, using a few buttons to set the device by entering "time now" into the system. Behind the scenes, more silicon and more metal. But many of the small components are battery operated. Battery production involves magnesium, nickel, lithium, cobalt and basalt. Their sources are scattered across the globe–in Canadian nickel mines and those in South-East Asia, Chinese graphite factories, new sites for extraction in Tanzania, Mozambique, and Madagascar. Processing of the raw material into usable form is concentrated in China. The Democratic Republic of Congo is the chief source for cobalt, with dramatically greater reserves than almost anywhere else in the globe except, perhaps, for Australia. Equally dramatic are accounts of the horrors and costs of cobalt mining to workers and environments. Lithium, essential for battery production, is expected to be in shorter supply than demand within a few years. Current industry assessments, to use euphemistic language, suggest adequate supply only for the short-term future.[53] New research into using bacteria to recycle lithium and other metals is just beginning to produce results that might be viable in recapture and reuse. It makes fascinating reading.[54]

The effects of mining any of the metals used in batteries varies, but none are benign. Research on the effects of living in proximity to a manganese mine shows deleterious effects on children as well as adults.[55] The National Institute of Health makes a distinction between "chronic toxicity" and "occupational exposure" and considers children's health within studies of the first. In an area of Ukraine where open manganese mines exist, more than a third of the pediatric population had skeletal deformities and impaired development. Photographs of the mines are dramatic. Huge scars of carefully terraced excavation in the surface of the earth show where machines pulverize and extract the black manganese layers, scattering powder into the air. The cranes and conveyers are so large that they dwarf the transport trucks that scoot around the ground being filled by equally overshadowed earth movers and scoopers. The cranes, easily twenty times the height of the trucks, move systematically across the open mine making piles of the raw material while filling the air with dust. The colors are the somber hues of earth pigments—deep blue grey, yellow-ochre, red-rust, and raw and burnt sienna. Fathers work the mine, run the equipment, extract the metals, and drive it away while their children lose cognitive ability as a by-product of their labors.

In investigating the resources required to extract even the most accessible raw material, we could turn our attention to the giant cranes and their operation. What is required to produce a mechanical object that is that large, engineer its workings, keep it oiled and mobile, design the motors that raise and lower the boom, run the pulleys and lines, swing the entire machine on its base? What size of manufacturing plant is required to make its gears? Cast its arms? Who tests the equipment in the course of the design and production? Trouble-shoots the problems? Attaches the fuel lines and engines and keeps the tanks filled with gas whose combustion drives the operations? More pollution appears as the hot engine exhaust spews out, releasing its thermal waste and volatile organic compounds into the air. The workers have head aches and tearing eyes, nausea, and a likelihood of developing lung cancer as a result of exposure.

So, for producing the tiniest, least conspicuous piece of the coffee maker, its battery-powered digital clock and batteries, sends extensive toxins into the air on a daily basis far from my kitchen, my coffee, and my cats.

The copper heating element: thermal energy and pastes
For the water in the coffee maker to get hot, it must be exposed to a concentrated source of heat.[56] What is heat, exactly, now that we stop to consider? When asked, the oracular Google

tells me that it is the "transfer of thermal energy" from one thing to another. But how does that actually occur? Particles—atoms, molecules, and ions—move around at different rates in solids, liquids, and gases. Think of these differences as the motions of people in an elevator that is almost fully packed. The range of motion is considerable, as well as the rate and variation of vibration and movements. Particles that move faster excite those that move slower, similar to what happens on a disco dance floor. Everybody speeds up. Until they slow down.

The heat in the coffee maker serves a few purposes. It gets the water hot enough to rise through a one-way valve in the tube to the "shower head" where it is sprayed onto the coffee grounds. It keeps the coffee warm once it is in the canister. The heating element is also the outcome of high-skilled engineering. Metal wires, tubing, and insulation as well as specially designed clamps and cords are all present. A view of the heating element from above resembles an urban highway interchange with overlapping, intersecting, nested pathways for water and electricity. One part of this is called a "resistive" heating element and it is pressed against the warming plate. The element is surrounded by a special heat-conductive grease—or, as the suppliers call it, a "thermal conductive gap filler." Of course, what else? This goop is part of a family of pourable, spreadable, pumpable liquids or pastes that range in color and tone and display a wide spectrum of liquid and viscous properties. Some of these substances go by the poetic name of "potting compounds" and look like rich, nourishing soil. My next request to the oracle, to find out what these substances are made of, came back with the enigmatic statement that it consists of "a polymerizable liquid matrix" and various fillers with the capacity to be insulating (keep the heat where it belongs) and conductive (move it along efficiently).[57]

Start looking at the list of what thermal pastes are made of and it is like a tour of the metals in the periodic table—oxides and nitrides of aluminum, zinc, and even "micronized" silver particles suspended in a medium that is part silicon and part ceramic. Essentially, these are paste fillers of liquid metal. You'll be happy to know there are YouTube videos showing how to make this substance at home using some of your spare zinc oxide and silicone (like the paste you put on your nose to protect against the sun combined with the gooey white stuff used to seal shower tiles). Apparently, in an emergency, when a CPU in a computer is in urgent need of this thermal fix, cocoa butter, hazelnut cream, and/or toothpaste mixed with Vaseline can be substituted for the high-end stuff made by skilled technicians in high-end plants. Or so the self-help videos suggest. But rather than track the production of these items, let's go back to the heating element of the coffee maker, knowing full well that professionally made thermal paste is going to be the end-product of extraction, processing, and waste by-products.

The heating element is linked to a sensor system that provides thermal feedback, since otherwise it could over-heat, melt, and catch fire which is not considered good behavior for a counter-top appliance. What are the sensors made of? How are they wired into the on-off switch controls? Where are the fuses, installed for safety in case of radical overheating? What are they made of? And how and where and under what conditions are their parts mined, processed, transported, assembled.... I am exhausted by this ongoing examination of endlessly proliferating parts.

As to heat, that primal force, it is all about motion and excitement, like light and electricity. Atoms just want to have fun. Collisions transfer energy—from a faster moving object to a slower one, though in principle this is reciprocal, since the slower moving object transfers its slowness in return. Ponder that. Radiation carries heat through infrared waves—something we literally feel when near a fire or heat source (remember the inside of the thermos mentioned awhile back).

The field of thermodynamics has its modern origins at the end of the eighteenth century, but it was the 19th-century scientist James Clerk Maxwell who codified many of the principles for understanding heat as a form of energy. One of the statements in his 1871 *Theory of Heat* is that it "cannot be treated as a material substance because it can be transformed into something that is not a material substance, e.g. mechanical work." The profundity of this observation ripples through my mind as I consider the ways in which processes exist, not as substances, but as dynamic activities. The excitement of the atoms, ions, and molecules gets transferred, not as a thing, but as a level of activity. I am not sure if I want to calm the coffee maker down, soothe its over-excited circuits, or simply engage in an exchange with appreciation of the steady stream of atomic motions involved. The source of electricity connects the coffee maker to larger processes and systems.[58]

The electrical fuse, quite small in the case of the coffee maker, is another miracle of modern engineering but can still be made with 19th-century technology. The elements are a glass cylinder, metal cuffs, and a metal-strip filament that carries charge until it gets too hot, too over-stimulated, or suffers from a sudden burst of energy. Fuses are referred to as "sacrifice devices" because once they are "blown" by having current blast through that exceeds their "breaking capacity" they cannot be repurposed. Fuses are made of metals and glass, sometimes with a filament encased in porcelain, fiberglass, mica laminates, or pressed fiber instead of glass. Their surfaces screen printed or stamped with miniscule information showing the ratings of their voltage limits and other features. These are small, even miniaturized, objects usually the size of a couple of vitamin capsules or the plastic cylinder of current COVID tests. The industry in which they are manufactured and operate is subject to national and international standards because they are so crucial to safety. But every minute marking on the fuse connects it to laws and statutes that regulate an industry through codes of compliance. The social infrastructure of this has its own complexity, history, and elaborate rules. This just for the tiny fuse, not even visible, that is embedded somewhere out of sight in the wiring of the base of the coffee maker.

The heating element itself is made of a metal alloy—a combination of nickel, copper, iron or chrome. The nickel alloy, to take one, is manufactured in silvery-grey bars of semi-shiny substance. The manufacturing process, the industry advertisements state, increases various properties like "weldability" and "ductility" and enhances "corrosion resistance" over time.[59] One manufacturer suggests that the life expectancy of the nickel alloy might be twenty-five or thirty years. What happens to it after that? Decay? Dementia?

Once again, these manufacturing processes are depicted in diagrammatic form, as if no human intervention played a role in the series of steps from melting ingots to hot forging, rolling, coiling, drawing, annealing, forming and performing "shape memory treatment" on the metal. Machines are shown in schematic form as well in industry diagrams, as if they were generic, made of spindles, basins, stamping, and boiling containers. And the ingots of metal that go into the heating element? Those perfect units of raw material—their life cycle of extraction is completely erased. Ingots appear fully formed in industry diagrams, ready for processing into any shape required. Magic. But each stage of highly industrial activity involves massive input of energy, output of heat, gases, wastes, and specialized equipment that is itself produced through complex lifecycles and processes. This is becoming repetitive.

The heating coil is insulated and also secured with various brackets, screws, braces, and bits of metal and plastic. Above it is the warming plate, the metal disk that distributes and holds heat to keep the coffee at drinking temperature. There, between the metal plate and the heating element is the thermal grease for which, it seems, I can substitute toothpaste, Nutella, or a banana in a pinch—as per those self-help videos noted above. These parts are put together on an assembly line, usually far from the places where the individual components are made. There, in a large warehouse-type space, workers keep an eye on the product parts, measure inventory, make sure that shipments are correct, on time, and orders filled at the wholesale level for distribution. An espresso coffee maker assembly line machine capable of making about ten coffee makers can be purchased from a Chinese company for about $13,000. You could be hatching out whole families of coffee makers in short order if you wished—if you could get the parts shipped to you in time. There are even portable assembly line units so you could set up shop on vacation if you became obsessed with making more coffee makers. The documentation of the factories always shows vividly colored, shiny, metal materials lined up on industrial tables under bright clear light. Most of the coffee makers are manufactured in China. An interview with a young woman who had worked in successive factories doing assembly work complained of the low wages, hard work, and abusive supervisors.[60] The Chinese workers are as young as fifteen, live in dormitories under difficult conditions, are banned from speaking to each other while working, as well as being subject to other constraints and threats.

Finally, we come to the last part in the coffee-maker, the

thermostat. This is one of the most basic feedback mechanisms, an object that does not learn and has no memory, but whose operation nonetheless is the basis of many other more complex systems. A strip of "bi-metal" is designed to detect temperature and open or close the circuit. The bi-metal strip is a physical object and it works because it is composed of iron and brass, which have different rates of expansion when heated. Since iron expands less than brass, the strip bends and separates from the circuit, breaking the flow of current. When it cools and returns to an upright position, it completes the circuit again. Thermostats can also be made with liquid that expands with heat and contracts, thus using the actual level of fluid in a tube as a mechanism. Smart thermostats, not the kind in my coffee maker, have predictive capacities and can anticipate the point at which a particular temperature will be achieved in a system. Probably they can predict when my readers will run out of patience as well.

My coffee maker, with its molded parts, shiny plastic and smooth-brushed aluminum canister, is a marvel of complex contemporary engineering. I could replace it with a simple ceramic or plastic cone perched in a cup or jar, a washable and reusable filter, and pulverize my beans by hand in a grinder with a little drawer in its base. But instead, I grind the beans, fill the water reservoir of the automatic coffee maker, press the buttons, see the blue control button lights appear below the glow of the digital clock, and let the machine run while I feed the cats.

Part One: Making Coffee

Even with this detailed description, I forgot one thing, the "ready" beep! All sounds are made by vibrating a surface or object. Such a clear and simple statement. In electronic devices the characteristic beeping sound is produced by a vibrating magnet connected to a speaker to amplify the sound—a fly in a glass bottle hooked up to a trumpet. Electronic sounds are made from an electrical circuit and apparently, though the engineering is beyond my comprehension, they are in the form of what is known as a "square wave"—"more or less a pure tone with overtones."[61] They are cheap, very cheap, to manufacture which accounts in part for the ubiquitous presence of annoying sounds in our current lives. I silenced the beep on my machine, which is probably why I forgot it except as an afterthought.

Tired yet? We are nowhere near finished.

● ●

Half and Half: The animals appear
No cows stroll through my kitchen or yard, and I would have no clue about how to milk these animals, draw off the cream, pasteurize or homogenize the raw warm bodily substance into any of the dairy products I use. I

was in a cow barn, once, a long time ago, early in life. We were taken on a school trip to a long room where milking machines were attached and the characteristic flat-topped metal cans were hauled out into a refrigerated dairy. But like most of what underpins my daily life, I have no contact with the processes that produce the consumer goods on which I depend. I could survive without half-and-half of course, it is a luxury not a necessity, but at first glance I think it will be one of the least complicatedly produced components of my morning. Cows to kitchens, right? Well, of course, there is the packaging, storage, and transportation to consider, but before that—?

Cows and food, shelter, anti-biotics and health care, breeding and selection, and the expertise involved in maintaining the animals through their lifetimes—all of this is required for the animals to produce. With this comes methane, which contributes a hefty 7+% to greenhouse emissions in the United States.[62] Of this, only about 1.4% is from what is referred to as "enteric" fermentation, by which is meant the gas released by the animals, their intestinal off-gassing so to speak

The costs of dairy are nothing like those of meat as a food source. At every step up the food chain, the ecological cost increases.

Milk production: Hazards in the dairy
My half and half is processed and packaged in California.

Diagram 11: Half and half

Cows are trough fed in confined conditions, brought into the milking area and spray washed as they walk. A milking apparatus is attached to their udders. The milk flows into tanks and is checked for diseases and contaminants and then heated in the pasteurization process. The cows produce their own waste in solid, liquid, and gas form. This is processed on-site as it drops, is collected, laid out to dry, put into methane-producing fields, and re-used. Dried dung becomes bedding, liquid waste becomes fertilizer, and gas is used in cooking and other processes.

The paper carton is probably sourced from materials as much as a half a world away, but the dairy product it contains is from cows in the Central Valley. A single cow, to be viable, needs about 1.5-2 acres of land for grazing.[63] This is known in the industry as the "forage inventory" essential for success since the costs of feed to substitute for this substantially increases the costs of maintaining the animals.

California, with its huge agricultural industry, is the major producer of milk in the United States. All those images of Wisconsin and its barns, the cheeses, and farms are real, but the scale is outstripped by California. Now struggling with drought and water shortages, the state is trying to maintain its agricultural strength.

I take a virtual tour of a California dairy farm. The video plays happy music, the rapid strumming of a guitar underscores the aerial view of a large collection of bare fields and long rows of sheds where the cows are sprayed with water to keep them cool. "Cow comfort level" is a major concern of the farmers since it links directly with productivity.[64] The cows are milked in a "milking parlor" which accommodates one hundred and sixty cows at a time. Cows have to be milked three times a day. Milk used to be geographically constrained, a local product. Before refrigeration, dairy cow owners brought a cow to the door of consumers so they could have the milk fresh in a pail.

How quickly we forget, if we ever knew, how recent

refrigerators and even ice boxes are and how precarious the preservation of food was before these technologies existed. Now I take the half-and-half carton from the shelf in my refrigerator where it sits flanked by a jar of rarely used mayonnaise, another of capers, and other generally neglected but long-shelf-life condiments. The half-and-half is used daily, and when I purchase the pint carton, I always look for the longest-out expiration date. My consumption rate is slow, and making it through a pint before the white liquid curdles in the coffee is a private race against an invisible ticking clock.

The happy music video continues, showing huge stainless steel milk tanks where thousands of gallons are kept cold with "plate coolers." Pipes and machines are everywhere, along with floor grating, automatic systems that are all running on electricity. The employees drive to work, their trucks and cars littering the open space along the buildings that house the milking operation. Dozens of open sheds with metal roofs provide the feeding stations for the cows who have a constant supply of hay and other foodstuffs. The hay is stored under its own open shed roofs, all metal, all peaked to increase water run-off in the wet season. This is California. In other parts of the country and the world, the shelter needs are likely different.

As the cows come into the milking facility, their undersides are sprayed by a robotic hose or sprinkler track. Then they find their spot in the stall, are wiped, and have the milking apparatus attached to their udders by human hands. After the milk stops running into the tube, someone removes the apparatus and sprays the cow again. The cows are tested constantly and separated out if they have any illness. After all cows are finished, the gate opens and they file back to their feeding troughs. Constant washing goes on, and the amount of running water is staggering. Estimates are that 900 pounds of water is needed for one pound of cheese.

Cows are ruminants, very effective at transforming grain, vegetable matter, and fiber into food and then creating food in return. In California, the farms use carrots, onions, almond hulls and other matter that has been rejected for market or is a byproduct in another production stream. Even by-products from producing ethanol can be fed to cows… along with whey, a liquid leftover from making cheese (Little Miss Muffet ate it too). Food waste from muffins, bread, tortillas is processed in the "bakery" on the farm and used to feed the cows. Other terms come into play in descriptions of food for the cows: silage and sorghum. These are esoteric materials, the stuff of agricultural science and animal husbandry, far from the world of urban consumption.

Once collected, the milk is sped from the milking barn to a processing facility, keeping it cool the whole way. The cream is separated from the milk with a centrifuge that spins the liquid around in a vast vat. Three different streams—low fat, full milk, and cream—are sent to separate tanks. Then the different streams are combined to make half and half and other milk products.

The milk must also be pasteurized, which means heating it to kill bacteria and give it a little extra shelf-life. Smaller, older farms use a slow heating method that brings the milk to about 150 degrees for three-quarters of an hour while newer plants bring it to a high-temperature for just a few seconds. The economics of small and large farm production is fraught with inequities and challenges, but food safety is a major concern. The milk is heated from steam in the walls of stainless steel vats in which the liquid is stirred constantly to be sure all milk gets pasteurized. Then it is homogenized so that the cream, which is lighter, doesn't separate out. Cream formed a buttery top in the neck of the glass bottles delivered to our house when we were children.

But, here is a curious fact. For the cream to stay evenly distributed in the milk its molecules have to be broken down by high pressure pistons. Battered cream molecules are in my half and half. For low-fat dairy, the cream is separated out, kept to be made into butter. Or, for half and half, it is mixed back into milk. A plant-based (sugar) additive from red seaweed, carrageenan, helps to emulsify the half and half and keep its texture consistent. Some research has shown it causes inflammation and is even linked to colon cancer. Details.

The dairy industry is filled with chemicals. Non-organic milk often contains high levels of growth hormones, antibiotics, and pesticides.[65] Bovine growth hormones are added to feed or injected into cows. For a shock, go to the Beyond Pesticides website and look at the list of chemicals they monitor in the food industry.[66] The list is hundreds of entries long. Their discussion makes clear that commercial milk production is chemical-intensive.

The list of pesticides that appear frequently in commercial milk is only about a half a dozen items long, but take the first one, atrazine, an herbicide, labelled toxic, and associated with cancer, endocrine disruption, kidney/liver damage, developmental problems, and other issues. It is used to control weeds in crops like wheat and grasses and so ends up in the food chain. And while atrazine is only found in about a quarter (!) of commercial milk samples, diazinon is found in about 60%. An insecticide, diazinon is sprayed on almost every fruit or vegetable imaginable and creates disruption in every human system from endocrines to nerves and blood.[67] Nice. These substances also disrupt the animals' systems—diazinon is toxic to birds, bees, fish and other aquatic organisms. Consuming organic dairy products provides some protection, but pesticides and toxins travel through air, water, and other routes of contamination into the feed of even the most carefully cared-for animals.

The happy videos that show these processes never address the cleaning techniques for disinfecting equipment. Nor do they show sick cows and dying ones. Most dairy cows get worn out or "spent" after about five years of high-level milk production. When this happens, and they can't produce milk, they are simply slaughtered and turned into beef products. Other aspects of the treatment of cows—lame or sick cows—is too gruesome to describe, frankly, and occurs at a scale that is sickening to contemplate.[68]

Manure: Managing methane gas
The images I find of dairy farms in California all picture the cows standing in their lines at the feeding troughs, under tightly-stretched shade tents. Cows stand around, eat, and get milked. Maybe they share stories while they are together, but it's hard to say. They produce manure constantly, and so a system of water flushes the alleys, rushing around their feet, sending a mix of manure and liquid into a big concrete pit. A system for processing this constant flow has to be in place, so now imagine pipes and railings surrounding a pit where a pump sends the liquid up into a "separator." More energy use, more specialized equipment. The manure separator is a platform with railings above a system of pipes where solid matter is extracted, and squeezed as dry as possible by rollers that pass over a screen. The liquid is collected while the carpet of solid matter (squeezed cow dung) flows down through a final squeeze from the rollers before being released. A constant rain of brown solid matter falls from the gridded screen. This dries into soft piles of fresh brown fiber that will be used for bedding the cows. The separating platform is high off the ground, several storys at the least, and offers an unobstructed view of the farm, including the wide open space where the solid manure is spread to dry. The tall piles of bulldozed manure are covered with tarps to keep dry.

Part One: Making Coffee 203

The liquid remains of the process are sent through a long trough so that any leftover solid matter can drop out. Then the liquid goes into a mechanical digester that purifies the methane for use as a gas. This involves first collecting it in a huge outdoor pond that is covered in heavy tarps that resemble a giant zip-lock bag. The system constantly monitors the flow rate in and out of the holding pond to optimize gas removal. A condenser that looks like a heavy trash can removes remaining liquid and a cooler brings the temperature of the gas down. Dairies cooperate on this process, and so liquid is often piped out and collected in a central location that makes purification more efficient. There the hydrogen sulfide, carbon dioxide and other impurities are removed. This process keeps the methane from escaping into the atmosphere and makes it available for any purpose for which natural gas is used—cooking, home heating, and so on. Miles and miles of pipes connect the dairy farm with the natural gas company that distributes the gas. Meanwhile, the manure water is recycled for irrigation and for the flushing activity that brings the cows' waste into the system. This is a pretty efficient system overall, but is more infrastructure consumers rarely see or know about.

About a quarter of the world's land is used for grazing animals. George Monbiot, author of Regenesis, makes the claim that pasture-fed beef and lamb do the most ecological damage of any farm product. The animal grazing produces only a miniscule amount of the world's protein—approximately 1%. The biomass of cattle, sheep, pigs is more than twenty times that of all wild animals on the planet but causes radical land degradation. But, as far as affluvia, it is the methane and nitrous oxide (laughing gas) the cattle give off that is the worst contributor to eco-disasters.[69] Not funny at all. To modify the methane levels in cow fermentation, certain additives can be put into the feed that change the chemistry of the digestive process. Strange to imagine that we are trying to alter cows' digestion on a mass scale in order to keep milk production from producing so much pollution.

Interestingly, milk consumption has declined by 40% in the last fifty years in the United States as plant-based options have proliferated.

The carton: From flatland to container
Before leaving the half and half, we have to briefly address the paper container it comes in. Square, peaked, and carefully shaped, the milk carton is a wood product like the coffee filter. Recall that in paper production, wood chips are processed into softened fiber—visualize a mass of dry, hard, tough flakes of wood being submerged in warm water and bathed in chemicals that break down the cellulose (as per the earlier discussion of paper production). After that, oxygenated chlorine is applied to bleach the fiber into a nice light colored pulp, something like white oatmeal. In these few sentences, we are already multiple stages into a heavily industrial process that uses lots of water and lots of chemistry, all of which produces off-gassing through evaporation and waste cycles. The thick pulp gets passed between rotating disks that grind it even finer.

Part One: Making Coffee 205

Now we have a smooth white pulp that flows easily into a paper-making machine, with an endless wire or plastic belt that produces a continuous roll. The water seeps out, the damp pulp gets squeezed between rollers and then dried. Some of this was described with the coffee filter.

The automated "Fourdrinier process" for paper production was invented in the 19th century (actually 1799 in France by someone named Louis Robert) to make long, continuous rolls. These were essential for meeting demands of motorized presses and without this technology—and the processing of wood pulp into paper (instead of cotton rages, used previously)—the printing industry would not have been able to become fully automated. Hand made sheets were too labor intensive, and too irregular, to be useful in the kind of high speed printing required by newspapers, mass market publications, books, journals, and the wide array of posters, flyers, playing cards and other printed materials. Now the machines are fully automated.

Interestingly, the labelled diagrams I find bear the imprint of their moment of origin in the names of the key parts. The terms breast roll, guide roll, tension roll, save-all tray and dandy roll, for instance, speak to me of another era when the relation of human motions to machine design was more apparent. The Fourdrinier machine that makes the paperboard embodies the aesthetics and engineering of an era when mechanization strove to imitate human gestures. Few imagined, two hundred years ago, a scale of production that would devastate vast forests or produce so much waste that it threatens the ecosystems from which the wood itself is taken. Or "machines" whose operations have little to do with imitating movement.

To picture the paper-making process, imagine the sound of slurry moving through metal troughs, the click and whirr of the rollers turned by their well-machined gears and coordinated motors. Now visualize some specific details involved in the operation. Strips of metal keep the slush from overflowing into the gears and guardrails, though looking at the pictures I am unsure of the scale of the trough of pulp. At first I thought the machine was the size of a gurney or operating table—or, at its largest, a newspaper printing press. Then I see the stairs and open-grate platforms and realized this machine is more the size of a football field. The amount of pulp that flows through these rollers and is pressed against the screens to become paper is a staggering non-stop digestive process. It is as if a giant maw were devouring northern forests without stop, swallowing the mass of cellulose and churning out paper pulp. Paper making is a messy process, wet and stinky, and the technical literature in the industry refers blithely to the phase of "de-watering" and drainage without giving any specifics about water recycling.[70] I remember visiting a paper plant once and being sickened by the smells.

In the last half-century, technical improvements in the machinery have involved strategic research into creating pressure and analyzing the dynamics of specialized wiper blades that are a crucial part of the process. As in all industrial processes, a dive into the literature reveals a highly specific language and purpose-designed machinery. For instance, one technical study by a professor at the University of British Columbia, Richard Kerekes, published in 2017 in *Bioresources.com* contains these phrases: "As paper machine speeds increased over the years, control of the headbox jet became ever more critical." The only way to understand this statement is to know that the headbox is where the slush first enters the system and begins to flow over the screens. But the next sentence spirals into unknown territory: "In a pioneering study, Nelson (1960) found that in the absence of gravity effects, two dimensionless numbers governed jet contraction and angle of outflow: the ratio of the bottom lip extension to the slice opening, L/b, and the ratio of the slice opening to the size of the channel upstream, b/B." (2127) Never, in my wildest dreams of my early morning routine, could I have imagined that any part of the production of these most ordinary items, milk cartons, could have involved "dimensionless numbers." (These deal with ratios rather than explicit quantities, but still… there are hints of *The Twilight Zone* and I don't pretend to be able to decipher Nelson's research findings.)

Once the paper web rolls through the conveyor it is dried by being passed between steam-heated rollers. To be useful for making containers to hold liquid, the paperboard has to be waterproofed with a layer of molten polyethylene. Yes, molten. The paperboard is pulled through rollers that apply the polyethylene to both sides in a very thin film. After all, these are synthetic polymers and once they dry, their bonds are indissoluble in water. We've met polyethylene before, since it is one of the most commonly produced plastics and used everywhere in packaging. Long strings of hydrogen and carbon atoms, arranged as if for a formal dance, stretch their bonds in a continuous line, and form a layer of film on the paperboard that keeps the half-and-half from seeping through. Even that statement is an oversimplification since there are multiple layers, each serving their own purpose (reducing moisture penetration, or air, or retaining the oil in the liquid), even if they are laid down in one pass.

Of course, nothing is that simple, and though we will skip any more discussion of the chemistry of the polymer, and not bother to trace its production back to the extraction of raw materials, factories, processing plants, shipping, and so on, we will pause to think about forming the carton from these sheets of coated paper.

At this stage, the paper can still be rolled, but it is too wide to be useful for making milk cartons. A full-sized roll can be more than three meters wide, and the weight of these staggers the mind and threatens the bodies of those who handle them. Paper is delicate, and avoiding bumps and bruises is essential in the handling process. A dent from a drop or other impact can ruin a stack or a roll—as we all know from receiving a bumped book that has (barely) survived the postal system. Then the carton gets printed. In the case of my half-and-half, blue and purple are the colors involved, though current presses can print up to seven different colors at once. Every form of printing now has a digital front end and even if aluminum offset printing plates are used, the images on them are no longer created from film made in a darkroom and exposed to photosensitive surfaces that require lacquer and washout. Instead, they are made with a digital file and camera, more technology with its own development costs.

The information on the carton is largely banal—the product name, the brand, and some images. But wait, there are graphics! Two sides of the carton bear the product identity, declaring it is half-and-half, in my case, from Trader Joe's, with assurances that their cows "say no" to "GMO" and other interventions. Cow speak? Maybe they do tell each other stories.

The image is the same on both sides, in antique wood block style, of a milkmaid with a wooden pail, cap, and apron, pulling at the udders of a cow in a rural setting. Right. On the third side a text claims that this half-and-half is righteously produced and on the final side is the required statement of nutritional facts. These, too, could be subjected to analysis. Are the claims in the promotional statements accurate? And the nutritional information? Tracking the regulations, language, and the social, physical, chemical, scientific systems that go with assessing nutritional value would be another study across multiple disciplines. To read that nutritional label completely would lead us into chemistry labs, nutritionist literature, analysis of the caloric values of every consumable substance. Cultural issues arise as well: whose body metrics and what cultural standards are used to establish daily percentages—safe, required, recommended—of any of these components? An average man in North America? A woman in sub-Saharan Africa? A transgender gymnast in Siberia? The encoded assumptions and blind spots are everywhere in everything, unmarked and unannounced.

What about the inks for the carton? Food safe and non-toxic? But still permanent enough to last, un-smeared and un-faded, through the lifecycle of the carton? Where are these from and by what long journey do they arrive at the carton factory to be used in creating the two-color image of my half-and-half carton? The purples used in contemporary inks are mainly synthetic, not linked to the great tradition of Tyrian purple from snails developed in the ancient world to dye royal robes. In the 19th century, a whole new palette of colors emerged from chemical laboratories because it was easier to use mined substances than the plants and insects that had served earlier generations. The chemical formula for manganese violet, for instance, looks like a freight train composed of a series of box cars each containing the notations for phosphoric acid, manganese dioxide, and so on. This simply reinforces what is a continuing thread throughout this book which is that 19th and 20th century industrialization introduced manufacturing at scale across every sector of our lives, particularly in the developed world and at the expense of the developing nations.

Other studies of the carton would lead to a long list of people whose skills went into its production. Who did the design? On what machines and computers? Who created the fonts and the typefaces, the devices for output and system of proofing? What editorial crews and teams are behind the apparently straightforward text about the purity of the half-and-half and its safe and conscientious production? What order of command in the Trader Joe's

Part One: Making Coffee 211

hierarchy would be exposed if the text were followed from its first drafts through to the printing on the carton? What legal team had to review it before it was allowed to go to press? And who checked which regulations in the dairy industry or the Food and Drug Administration just to be sure all aspects of the package, contents, and statements were in compliance with USDA rules and regulations? Who sets those regulations at the Federal level? Is it Congressional lawmakers who determine the FDA guidelines? Are they laws or are they simply regulations created by a particular agency whose activity is overseen by—whom? And how often and on what schedule are these checked? Has this changed with the Supreme Court's recent decision to set aside the *Chevron* case that devalues professional expertise in regulatory agencies? And, for that matter, how often are the dairies inspected to be sure they are complying with federal and local regulations? And who pays for that? The taxpayer? The industries? The consumer? Are the food inspectors federal employees? Everything, everywhere, leads to elaborate complexity too interlocked and entangled to keep clearly in mind.

Once printed, the paperboard is scored and then cut with a die stamper (more metal work) into the correct shape.[71] This flat piece is known as a blank. Another machine that folds it, seals it with heat, and makes the seams that keep the carton watertight (more electricity and adhesives). Then the flat, seamed, blanks are shipped off to the dairy where a "forming machine" turns them into three-dimensional objects.

This operation also has its specialized terminology as the blanks are sucked onto mechanical arms, or "mandrels." These snap the flat carton open and fold it along the score lines, overlapping the bottom flaps which are then heat-sealed into place. The half-and-half is put into the carton before the top is sealed so the cartons march to the filling area on their conveyor belt, neatly aligned and mechanically spaced so that their openings fall directly under the release spout. All of this is automated, so consider the way volume is controlled and measured to assure that every carton gets the same exact amount of liquid. How is this done? By a timer? A lever? A feedback mechanism? A belt of a certain length?

The top of the carton is sealed into a gable shape using heat and the polyethylene coating already present which bonds to itself. Then, in a last nod to the ephemerality of all things, the little cartons are date-stamped. Their pointed peaks roll though a press that prints their projected expiration date. Doomed to mortality as they are from the moment of their creation, they pass into the world on trucks and into the stores where they are taken from the shelves by the consumers who, like me, have reached for the cartons for years without a thought for the lifecycle of their production or contents.

● ●

Part One: Making Coffee   213

Coffee Cup: Ceramic durability
Thirty-odd years ago, I received a gift of a pale green coffee mug with a decal image of a painting of a cat on it. Since then, I have used it daily except when travelling. My morning coffee and the mug are bonded in my mind, as if the feel of the light ceramic and tone

of the glaze contribute to the taste of the coffee. The color I aim for when I put in the half and half is carefully calibrated to that of the mug.

Issued by the Metropolitan Museum of Art in a limited edition, it is no longer available. The original image, titled *Cat Watching a Spider*, was painted between 1888 and 1892 by a Japanese artist, Oide Toko. The curve of the cat's whiskers and arc of the spider's legs echo each other. The cat's directed focus organizes the entire picture in a tight cone of vision around the edge of a screen where the spider moves unaware. The soft grey-green tones of the painting are only interrupted by the bright orange and blue pattern of the scarf the cat wears (go figure), but otherwise, the color remains within a small range of values punctuated by the white paw of the crouching feline and black edge of the screen. The action in the image is suspended between patience and predation, its resolution unclear in the moment. But as a depiction of concentrated attention it is perfect for morning coffee.

The original image was painted in ink and color on silk and remediated multiple times before it appeared on my mug. The production details of that original painting, including the manufacture of silk and the creation of inks and colored pigments, are too far removed from the ceramic mug production to be relevant to the analysis here. They are not present in my kitchen.

Part One: Making Coffee

Instead, focus on the mug itself and attention to clay, a naturally occurring material. I think of river banks and lake beds, and of soft moist earth squishing through my toes. Clay feels like a primal substance, able to be grabbed directly from the source, massaged into shape, and fired in fairly basic conditions. Right? Maybe originally, but not now. Everything is far more complicated than in those early days scooping muck by the river bank and baking things in the oven.

My mug is ceramic and made of white, high-quality material probably kaolin, mined in the United States as well as many other places. The earliest ceramics—clay fired to make it hard and waterproof—have been traced to Czechoslovakia some thousands of years before they appeared in China, where expertise in the craft excelled. The ancient Near East, Egypt and other sites of ancient culture contain evidence of ceramic production since about 10,000 years ago. That makes it as old as agriculture and urban society.

At the industrial scale, ceramic production begins with mining operations in open pits using earth movers and scrapers, back hoes and power shovels—the full roster of machines capable of physically transforming earth. As so often, we begin with extraction. Watching a mining operation from a distance suggests giant earth-eating creatures consuming the landscape in their shovel mouths by means of their mechanical reach. Dust rises. The sound of earth grinding and falling fills the air along with the hum and beep of truck motors backing up and stopping, moving forward and turning around. The slicing of the earth reveals the many layers of sediment, each slightly different in color from the others, a layer cake of deposits that can be pulverized, washed, cleaned and turned into a soft paste for the manufacture of everything from floor tiles and bricks to coffee mugs and lamps. Like any open mining, the operation creates a large raw gash in the earth with steep ramps winding down into the pit area. The shovels fill and wind upward, depositing their heavy load in trailers to be hauled off to local refineries for crushing and grinding.

To identify the clay deposits, companies drill in a systematic pattern. They mark out an area with a grid, send a shaft into the earth, and test before they begin the heavy work of removing the clay. The long columns of the drills remain visible, tendrils reaching into the earth. One site in California produces a high quality kaolin clay, white and fine, perfect for ceramics like my mug. The blinding white strata are visible in the hillside, stripes as vivid as chalk in the sedimentary layers of earth tilted up by the action of tectonic plates. Pipes, water, steel scaffolding and custom-designed technical infrastructure are all integral to the mining operation, particularly for hydraulic extraction. Workers wear respirators and heavy gloves. Before the material can be used, it has to be physically transformed, ground and dried. Sometimes it is filtered, "de-gritted," or

Part One: Making Coffee

bleached before being classified by size and quality. Each step of the process leaves some waste, piles of dry cast off dirt that throws dust into the air or fumes. No surprise.

I get curious about types of clay. The USGS (United States Geological Survey) informs me that six different clays are mined in the United States. These are used in a wide variety of industries that make everything from ceramic toilets to absorbent buffering materials, bricks, sanding and bonding agents.[72] The list is long. Kaolin, the clay used most in making dishware, is classed within the "refractory markets." These are defined as materials that are resistant to decomposition. They can resist chemicals, stand up to heat, and pressure and are often used in making high temperature and high pressure furnaces, kilns, and even reactors.[73] These are properties commonly associated with ceramics, of course, and different grades and textures. The term clay is applied to materials with very small particle size, but the generic term can include mixtures of minerals and crystals such as quartz and metal oxides. All clays have a strong affinity for water, which they can soak up easily.

But clay as it comes out of the ground needs to be ground very finely. The processing of what are called "high brightness" kaolin clays involves a "beneficiation process" that is also called "ultra flotation." These are terms invented by the industry and associated in some cases with patented processes.[74] They refer to the operations in which raw material is ground and turned into slurry, mixed with water and various agents that make physical and chemical changes so that the usable and non-usable elements can be filtered out. In one part of the process, particles are attached to air bubbles to assist in separation. Imagine the effervescence as these many bubbles burst on the surface of a large tank or flow. These are relatively recent industrial processes and "beneficiation" (which sounds like an act of blessing) has only been used industrially since the 1960s, though older methods of floatation processing have long traditions.

As in so many of the descriptions of industrial processes, the human factor disappears behind flow charts and diagrams in which one step leads to another as if it were purely mechanical. So, in the processing of kaolin, the crude substance goes through blending, water dispersion, degritting, fractionation, size reduction, floatation, high-gradient magnetic separation, oxidative bleaching, reductive bleaching, dewatering, drying, calcining and surface treatments.[75] That list, from an industry paper, would be interesting to study from the point of view of a few particles and their pathway from one vat or oven to another. What a journey that is, and how far the substance ends up from its original excavation site. The processes are like a series of spa treatments for the kaolinite mineral, which comes out bright white and shining. Through whose hands does it go?

Stoneware, earthenware, porcelain are all types of clay that go into ceramics, some heavier and cruder than others. But the kaolin for porcelain is considered the most regal

Part One: Making Coffee 219

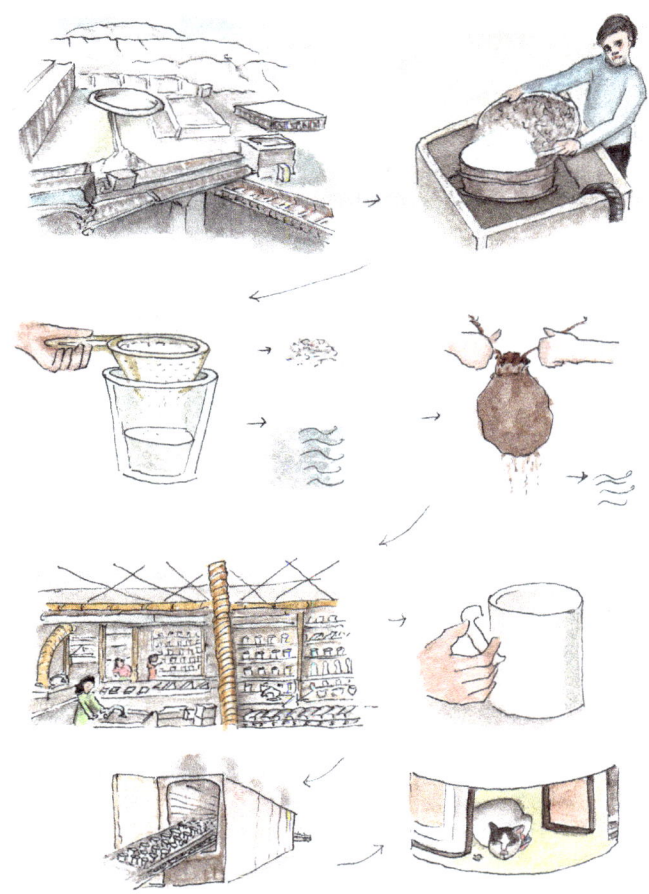

Diagram 12: Coffee cup

Kaolin clay, finely grained and white, is extracted from open pits. The clay is strained and washed to remove debris and the waste water and rocks are discarded. The clay is squeezed to remove excess fluid, then processed into shapes at a factory where workers assemble cups from parts, attaching handles. The ceramics are fired in a kiln at high temperatures and then a printed decal is attached and baked onto the surface.

of clays, its refined and delicate texture combines with strength and remarkable resilience.[76]

The clay for my mug will have been made at a ceramics plant in a large drum (capacity over 3000 lbs) where the clay powder is combined with feldspar, quartz (more mining), and water. When the substance comes gushing out, following the course of its trays and mechanical stream beds through the factory, it gets cast into the clay equivalent of ingots—little logs of moist clay. These are sliced and stuck into molds of glass and plastic. A human operator pulls down a mechanical arm that spins into the lump of clay, spreading it across the bottom and up the sides of the mold to make a cup. While the molds are washed and re-used, the still moist cups are sent to an operator who attaches their handles with a clay and water mixture known as slip. This bonds the parts together. In rapid movements, the operator presses the handle against a spinning wheel coated in slip, holds the cup against a guide, and pushes the handle into place trying not to distort its shape.

The mugs are hand-inspected one at a time for any flaws, bits of clinging clay or dust, and given a final scrape or wash if necessary. The tub of water is greyish, the hands of the operator covered in gloves, and the space is intimate, close, as each object is handled in turn. The mugs are dipped into a vat of glaze, or more than one, depending on color choices. The mugs and their glaze have to dry before they are put onto a conveyor belt and sent through a kiln at somewhere over 2000 degrees from which they emerge glazed and shiny, ready for packing and shipping.

But what of the other ingredients mentioned in the process? The feldspar, for instance, is a mineral, abundant in the earth's crust. Some is made as magma cools, formed under pressure and heat, but it is a primal element, abundant here and even on the moon and in meteorites. Think of the many crystalline beauties in the cases of a geologic display in the natural history museums. Feldspar contains alumina and silica, was produced through thermal expansion and contraction, melting oxides of various kinds (mainly potash and soda—potassium and sodium). All of this is geologic history, the story of our ancient past, surfaced in a mountainside in North Carolina, for instance, where the dry rocky crystals are easily accessible and seem to crumble out of the gash in the earth to be put into the clay of my mug.

But what of those abandoned mines? The strange ghostly zones where a pock-marked surface in the earth lies wasted and weather-beaten. Water seeps into the craters and scars where it breaks down the residual minerals. These are simply physical-chemical processes, the effect of rain water on rocks, but they release a chain reaction in which one compound changes simple water into an acid that then breaks down other substances and carries fluid waste laden with metals like copper, cadmium, and zinc into the local water supply. Working mines are regulated, their wastes tested and controlled, but abandoned mines are not. And in that cycle of neglect and negligence, out of sight and lacking oversight, persistent and deadly damage is done.

So the quick answer to the question of environmental impacts of feldspar mining is that it causes erosion, contamination of soil and water, wrecks bio-diversity, and also causes sinkholes.[77]

That mining process is far from my kitchen and my cup, though holding it in my hand, feeling the smooth surface of the glaze, I like to imagine that by using just one cup for more than three decades I have at least been conservative in my contributions to these industries.

Then, the images of the factory workers come back. My grasp on the cup is gentle, my motions slow, meditative and habitual. But the video of the factory workers haunts these movements, as I think of their repetitive activity, through the day, pulling the lever of the mold, attaching the handles, dipping the cup into glaze, loading the long planks that slide through the kiln. My luxury is bought from their efforts. And what of the larger features of that process—the long kiln through which the conveyor belt travels with its hoods and ducts removing gas and fed by heat. Where was that made, and by whom? Where does the gas come from to fire the oven, who created the pipes and insulation, the knobs and valves with their threaded screw mechanisms?

Part One: Making Coffee 223

Looking at the bottom of the mug, I see that it has a number stamped into the base, "978." This individual mug was from a limited edition, in fine Limoges porcelain, made by the company Phillipe Deshoulieres, which was founded two centuries ago and still employs three hundred people.[78] Their promotional page touts their efforts to increase sustainability in the way they fire their porcelain and try to reduce consumption of natural gas. The traditional patterns on their china are incredibly delicate and artful, providing a strong feeling of continuity across centuries and cultures. The website reeks of wedding registries and social protocols in which I never partake, but my mug is connected to these worlds through its manufacture.

The decal image of the cat on the mug has been put onto the ceramic through a transfer process. In earlier centuries, the process involved taking a copper plate engraving, printing onto paper, and rubbing the transferable ink onto the ceramic surface. Heat, soap, and sizing were also part of the process which culminated in the firing of the object at a high temperature. Now a laser print on decal paper from a digital copier is sufficient to create a color image that can be transferred. The slight edge of the decal is apparent on my mug when I look at it from an angle. I can tell by looking closely that the colors were made from CMYK printing inks—cyan, magenta, yellow, and black—based on a digital file taken from a scan of the artist's original painting.

224   AFFLUVIA

Tracking the creation of digital files, photographic processes, storage and methods of production and the whole digital printer apparatus is beyond my scope here. But a brief discussion of the CMYK inks seems in order, along with a description of the creation of decal paper.

The standard four colors of printers' CMYK inks each have their own complex chemistry. Ink comes in cartridges, plastic containers custom-fit to each printer model on earth. We've spent enough time with mold-made extrusion plastic to have a general idea of what goes into making those cartridges, and their flaps, metal chip cards, nozzles, and other features of the device. This will have to suffice since each of those components as well as the printer itself, would lead to another detour into extraction industries and manufacturing without covering new ground.

As a full color image, made in CMYK, the decal's hues are the outcome of a "subtractive" system that was developed in the early years of the 20th century.[79] The ability of these four pigments to produce almost every color is nearly inexhaustible (though neon or day-glo pigments are outside of their range). CMYK colors used in printing processes are pigment based (as opposed to RGB, which are light based and used in screen displays).

Printer inks for cartridges, like printing inks used on printing presses, are often oil based. They use linseed oil or soybean oil or the ubiquitous petroleum distillate.[80] By itself the mixture of pigments and oil would be too thick and viscous to use in almost any circumstance, let alone to produce the fine spray of droplets from an inkjet. So a whole host of other additives are mixed in: dispersents, resins, de-foamers, and even biocides and bacteriostats. The terms are suggestive. Imagine what they are doing.

The lifecycle of ink includes multiple processes, from creating the basic medium, whether water or oil based, grinding and refining the pigments, mixing and diluting the ink and then packaging it for transportation and consumption. The pigments? We touched on this before in the discussion of the ink on the coffee bag. Carbon black is a pigment with an ancient history. The cave painters mixed their charcoal dust with water and natural gums and resins, making this and the earth toned ochres and umbers among the oldest pigments of which we have a trace. Pigments are the non-soluble particles that give color to a substance by refraction or scattering of light.[81] The chemistry of pigments is complex, detailed, and includes knowledge of crystalline structures, physical properties, and the effects on optical phenomena. Wavelengths of scattering and subtraction, spectral reflection, and selective absorption, for instance, become terms in use in describing what occurs in the relation between pigments and light and our perceptual capacities. To manufacture any specific colored ink to specifications, an understanding of these dimensions of the physical-chemical foundations of optics and light is required. In industry publications, the specialized vocabulary approaches alchemy with discussion of "electronic transitions of ions" and the "hiding power of the pigment."[82] The hide-and-seek of addition and subtraction in the production of color on screens and on pages plays with the qualities of light in two distinctive modes, each of which has been studied in highly granular detail.

But where does that leave us with our knowledge of what goes into cyan, magenta, yellow, and black inks for the decal printer? Pursuit of this specific information leads down one research trail after another. I find an article on fundamentals of pigments in a physics classroom site where the terms *absorb* and *reflect* provide the basics of color operations. We remember this vaguely from some lesson in high school, that cyan, which is the "blue" pigment absorbs red light and reflects blue and green. But what does that really mean? How does it absorb it? Where does the light go that gets absorbed? Does the absorption heat up the surface while the reflection cools it down? Is this light conceived as waves? Or particles? So much of the world around me is a mystery in spite of my efforts at understanding.

Let's go back to producing ink pigments from organic materials (remains of living things), inorganic materials (minerals, rocks, non-living materials), and synthetic ones (made by chemistry and considered to have begun with the creation of mauve—which became a rage—when invented by William Henry Perkin in 1856).[83] Some of the older pigments were heavy metals, like cadmium red and lead white. These are toxic but also, to use another color term, *fugitive*—they fade when they interact with air and moisture. The PrintWiki offers a succinct account of pigments used in inks, making clear that these are particles suspended in a medium, not dyes that bond with it. The range of source materials is varied—for white the list includes sources that invoke other associations—with sunscreen and common household powders. They include titanium, zinc, calcium carbonate, and aluminum. The processes of production of color pigments begin with suspension of particles in water, filtering out, and drying into "presscake"—think of those pans of dried color in the elementary school watercolor sets. In other cases, the wet mixture is combined with oil, processed into a paste and then dried. Or—we could go on. Metals, minerals, rocks, and earthly substances extracted, processed, ground, and recombined provide the foundation of most pigments.

Take just one of these back through its production, a black pigment, the most common and one of the oldest—the carbon black mentioned above. Not made from wood charcoal or soot anymore, but instead, from that common source material, petroleum. The PrintWiki provides the basic story that this black pigment is produced by a process called "cracking" in which the petroleum molecules, subject to high temperature, have their carbon bonds weakened. Some substances boil off, others remain as a residue and these hydrocarbons are in turned burned.

As their flame condenses on a cool surface it produces a black pigment. This is much like the soot on the back of a chimney, or the bottom of a pot hung over a wood fire, just that at the industrial level it is made from petroleum.

Not much additional information is needed to imagine the drilling of crude oil and its transformation, distribution, and specialized modification in the vats, furnaces, and cooling areas of a factory where carbon black is manufactured. And the workers? And the fumes? The ducts and the hoods? Waste products from the high volume of heating and firing, cooling and condensation? Because carbon black is used extensively in black rubber tires—not just for color but as a reinforcing agent, it is produced in massive quantities. The temperature for combustion is between 2400-2800 F.[84] Think, just for a moment, of what a sentence like the following one (taken from an EPA document) really means: "In the oil furnace process […], an aromatic liquid hydrocarbon feedstock is heated and injected continuously into the combustion zone of a natural gas-fired furnace, where it is decomposed to form carbon black." The ghostly spirit of hydrocarbon is what remains.

The flow diagram for the process from oil furnace to final carbon details more than three dozen processes along the way from oil storage and preheating to quenching (which is what?) and filtering and vacuum clean-up. I do a detour to look up "quenching" and find this sentence on Wikipedia, "A variety of processes can result in quenching, such as excited state reactions, energy transfer, complex-formation and collisions."[85] This makes it sound like a high school prom.

As in most of these flow diagrams, no human beings are present in showing the production of carbon black. The representation of processes as merely mechanical erases the labor, exposure, costs, and damages. The EPA has distinct guidelines for regulating the "effluent" from these industries and governs direct and indirect discharges, but again, the language functions at a level of abstraction that seems designed to keep the human costs concealed.[86]

The pictures of the plant where carbon black is manufactured make it look more like an oil refinery than a factory. A large area of cleared ground, about a half a mile square, is dotted with storage tanks, smoke stacks, and massive amounts of pipe and corrugated steel sheds. The roofs show rust and many of the surfaces have a smudged patina as if they were coated with a light sheen of carbon dust. The pollutants subject to regulation come from four areas—the furnace, thermal process, channel process, and lamp process. To gain a little bit of insight into what these are, I read through the EPA government documents from 2018.[87] This leaves me shockingly unenlightened. The language of the document is filled with phrases like "new source performance standards" but provides no information about the specifics of the industry.

In pursuit of information, I go to Carbon-Black.org. Here I find out a little more, though I have to read through the technical jargon to imagine what it means that "heavy aromatic oils" are used as "feedstock." I guess the oils are the petroleum products and that "aromatic" might mean they have a heavy odor though nowhere is there an indication of whether this is pleasant, unpleasant, or polluting. "Feedstock," I assume, is what kickstarts the carbonization process. These substances get put into a "heavy gas stream" that is made by burning other fuels (also fossil). At this point it "vaporizes and then pyrolyzes" so that microscopic carbon particles are formed. Pyrolyzing, it turns out, is simply the term for decomposition of something at a high temperature—as in cremation only even more extreme. These microscopic particles have to be captured, filtered out of air, steam, or water. Carbon monoxide and hydrogen, left over from the process, are recycled as much as possible to be used as fuels to continue to process.

The Carbon-Black site says nothing about pollution or environmental damage, but does have a gallery of highly professional photographs that show the range of products from cables, wires, batteries, agricultural irrigation, steering wheels, pipes, black plastic hangers and picnic ware, to coatings of all kinds and tires. These brightly lit and colorful photographs are the visual equivalent of the happy music that is played on documentary videos of industrial manufacturing as workers repeat motions endlessly in their coordination of bodies and machines.

The Wiki page is more direct, suggesting that exposure to the dust of carbon black might well be carcinogenic, particularly if inhaled (as opposed to sprinkled on oatmeal?). To prevent over-exposure, workers are supposed to wear sufficient protective respiratory apparatus and other gear. OSHA and NIOSH both set limits, legal and recommended, on exposure levels. Studies in Germany and the UK showed elevated mortality levels among these workers while studies carried out in the US did not. Different math? The industry is closely watched by economists and investors who see great potential for super-growth in market.

Once the pigment is made, shipped, and included in the toner cartridge, it is ready to be used in printing onto the transfer paper to create decals, among other things. The dense, absorbent color of that carbon black is familiar to us all, and the intensity of toner powder is greater than any water-based ink or even paint pigment. The dryness of the toner powder makes it absorb light without reflection or refraction, giving it a potent aura. Pigment names are also subject to regulation. The International Color Consortium is the agency whose mission is to promote vendor-independent color management systems. This industry has its own conferences, professional guidelines, and specifications, including a "Perceptual Reference Medium Gamut."[88] The details of this document once again boggle the mind with its technical language and demonstration of expertise.

Many people know an enormous amount about color, about pigments, light, ink, paint, and other media and are committed to keeping standards in place. They work with the ISO, International Standards Organization, to assure that color has consistency and authenticity. Among the challenges they address are those of working digitally where the integration of hardware (printing with pigment) and software (seeing light on a display and transforming it into ink values) has to be managed. Both nomenclature and measurement are challenges. Color names have many cultural resonances as well as market implications. CMYK colors do not venture into the trendy realms of apricot, blueberry, saffron, and storm, but remain as close to a single ongoing standard as possible, continuing the printing industry's commitment. That way the four-color printing process can be used consistently. CMYK is a sequential printing process in which one ink color is laid on top of the other in one wet-on-wet sequence. So the decal of my little cat and spider was originally printed in this way, not by mixing inks for each and every color in turn.

In the end, it is the structure of the pigment at the molecular level that is responsible for its color production. The physical arrangement of hydrogen, carbon, and other elements is responsible for the capacity to absorb or reflect light of different wavelengths. And for color to be produced, these must be in the visible area of the spectrum, or close to it. The specific molecular form is what determines the way the light is absorbed or not whether the pigment has existed since antiquity or been created yesterday in a lab.

This is as far as I will go with describing the components of the mug and their sources and processes of manufacture. As to the off-gassing involved in these many industrial operations, it is multiple in its outputs, types, and effects.

We have arrived at the end of Part One, Making the Coffee.

● ●

Part Two: Feeding the Cats

While the coffee brews, I pick up the cats' bowls, and open an aluminum pop-top can of wet food. The full-color paper label has a photo of a happy kitty reaching a paw upward. The brownish color-toned background signals the turkey flavor of the "paté" the felines are about to receive. The list of ingredients is long, but gives no indication of the manufacturing processes by which this familiar item appears in my hands. So far, so good. Then I start to investigate. What I find out is not pretty.

The can: Punched and rolled
The cat food can generates a rush of associations. Cat food. I love my animals. I am that cliché, a senior single woman living with her two cats. I spoil them as much as is reasonable, catering to their whims and tastes. In return, they are committed to complete disinterest in any human food–with

the single exception of butter, which Coco, the luxury cat, consumes with great pleasure. Cleo disdains.

What goes into the production of the cat food, can, and label? Paying attention first to the manufacture of the can, I find out that aluminum (already encountered in the glass jar lid and coffee canister) is almost entirely recyclable, unlike some plastic and synthetic rubber, and so it is a far more sustainable material, in principle. But whether its production can keep up with demand is a question. Used in automobile manufacturing, as well as packaging, it is light, strong, and versatile. Aluminum prices rose almost twenty percent on the world market between October and December 2020, and in the following year rose another fifty percent.[89] What does that indicate about supply and demand?

I'm staring at the cat food can's perfect round form whose bottom is imprinted with concentric circles that create very regular ripples leading to the well-turned rim, short sides, and the pull top cover. Such an ordinary item. One can a day is consumed at my house. At the cost of about a dollar retail, the can itself has to be a minimal part of the price.

The process of mining bauxite, the aluminum-rich ore, and smelting it has already been described. But the story of how a can is made from sheets adds another dimension not yet discussed. Just getting the aluminum from the ore absorbs considerable amounts of human activity (mining), transportation (shipping), processing using heat, pressure, energy, and water. As we already saw, the aluminum is turned into ingots that are processed through heavy rollers that transform them into thin, flexible sheets, just the way nuggets of pie dough become a crust with the aid of a pie pin. Variation in the cooling process results in different degrees of strength. Any sheet that is less than .0008 of an inch is considered "foil," another familiar material.

Those aluminum sheets get turned into heavy rolls, about nine tons apiece. Consider things that weigh a ton—a small "smarte" car, two grand pianos, a large moose, and, uh, apparently, whale testicles (but we will leave that aside)—and understand that the shiny metal roll of aluminum is nine times that weight and imagine trying to move it from spot to spot (like moving nine female cows at once….). But for the can to be stamped, the roll has to be maneuvered into place on a large press through which it unfurls, subject to the rapid impact of a punch that cuts rounds from the sheets. These shoot out, perfect circles, that are then bent upwards into a small cup to begin to form my cat food can. Depending on the final purpose, the proportions are determined in advance so that in the next phase the circular cup, already shaped, is pulled out to become a cylinder. In the case of the cat food can, the wall of that cylinder is not too high, but the process is basically the same as in the case of a soda can, which becomes light, elegant, with a "neck" and a "lip" bent over the top. The lip of the cat food can will be used to attach the pull top with its ring of smoothed and bent metal (made separately), into which I can put my fingers without damage. The remaining parts of the sheet—like cookie dough after the shapes are cut out—gets rolled up, compacted, and fairly effectively re-cycled. The aluminum in my can might have gone through several such cycles to arrive as the artifact in my kitchen, its top snapping off cleanly as I pull it back.

But that can whose manufacture we are tracking is not yet ready for my fingers. After being formed, it gets washed with hydrochloric acid, then water, then varnished a bit here and there, coated on the inside to keep the food substances from interacting with the aluminum. By the time it is finished, it has gone through more baths than the cats take in a day, or two, and certainly far more pressure.

Now ready to do their job, the cans are shipped to the factory where the cat food is made. For transport, they are loaded on pallets made of wood, part of the vast deforestation activity integral to industrial activity from home-building and papermaking to fast food packaging at a grand scale. Roped and confined with plastic to keep them in place, and belts to prevent slippage, the cans are on their way. We will follow them there to get an idea of what goes into the mix.

● ●

Part Two: Feeding the Cats

The food: Unimaginable ingredients
Now we are at the cat food factory. Vast quantities of meat and meat by-products—tuna, mackerel, chicken, beef, and even lamb, duck, goose, and shrimp are being offloaded from trucks. These are largely the parts of animals that humans won't eat or that can't be packaged and sold. Heads. Feet. Intestines. Lungs. Udders. Spleens and cheek meat. Sinews. This is ground up and mixed with grains—wheat, corn, soybean and barley—some minerals, and some protein and fiber are added. Less common knowledge is that much of the meat in pet food is recycled from euthanized house pets. More than 5 million dead pets were sent to the euphemistically named "rendering" plants. These materials only show up in the ingredients as "bone meal" or "meat" and are not otherwise identified.

Most of the other animal by-products, so-called, are collected from slaughter houses and processing plants as well as at independent sites that collect carcasses. Grease and blood, feathers, fur, bones and tails come from feedlots and farms, and animal shelters. At the plants, which are operated with supervision by USDA Food Safety and Inspection Services, health and safety standards must be maintained. The plants render the meat and extract various substances like fat in the form of tallow, grease, and ground or processed meat. These end up in soap and feed, but also are a source of essential fatty-acids in the cat food. Full cycle.

Diagram 13: Cat food

Meat and meat by-products arrive at the factory loading dock. They are inspected for bacteria and other substances that might cause harm. The meat products put through a grinder and then a large tank where the fat and edible materials are separated. Waste water is discarded and flows away. The meat paste is mixed with colorants, spices, flavor-enhancing substances, and preservatives, then sent through sieves and slicers to become chunks, threads, or smooth paté. This is put into the aluminum cans, which are sealed before the printed labels are attached.

The rendering process of the flesh involves trimming the fat, putting it through a grinder, then into a tank where it is melted, and spun in a centrifuge to pull the fat and water away from disposable materials. A fat tank collects edible materials while a sludge tank sends the unusable portions to a wastewater treatment facility. Along the way, the industry claims, no cooking vapors are emitted directly into the air.[90] So where do they go? A far less genteel, more toxic process is used for rendering meat into inedible products like fertilizer. For these processes, the flesh is sent directly from a receiving bin into a crusher and then moved through continuous cookers, condensers, drainers, presses, and storage tanks with VOC (Volatile organic compounds) and PM (Particulate matter) emissions at multiple points in the process. These are not part of the cat food production, so we can let this go for the moment.

At the meat processing plant, the loading dock and delivery areas are stained with fat and blood. Piles of flesh, not rotting yet, are shoved around by small lift vehicles, shoveled into industrial vats and metal tubs, washed and sprayed, boiled and compressed in huge vats piped and electrified, shining with chrome and baked enamel paint surfaces. Pulleys and hoses, conveyor belts and chains, hooks and various devices to pick up and move flesh before it decays are everywhere. Someone operates these. But even without rot, the odor is overwhelming, the smell of blood and dead flesh thickens the air. The number of pollutants in the VOCs is enormous, organic sulfides and carbons that create a stench near the plants are all regularly pumped into the air. Short-term effects are mainly irritation of the respiratory system and organs. Long-term?

Considerable research goes into cat food manufacture. Apparently, cats need amino acids added to their food since they can't extract it themselves. They also benefit from vitamins A, B, C, D and E and need various minerals added as supplements to their food, like zinc and fatty acids. In fact, pet food is far better balanced for nutrition than most food in school cafeterias or lunch programs, let alone fast food meals. As for the kibble I am putting in their bowls at the same time, after it was mixed and processed, it had heat-sensitive vitamins sprayed onto it along with fat—making it the tasty junk food of the cats' diet. But let's stick with the wet food coming out of the can.

AAFCO – Association of American Feed Control Officials–regulates labelling and ingredients. Senior cats and kittens have their own nutritional requirements. So do cats with kidney disease, which is very common. In the US there are more than 300 manufacturers of pet food and they make 7 million tons of pet food every year and feed about 130 million cats and dogs. This averages out to about 100 lbs of food per year per pet, though of course that ranges widely depending on size.

Once that rendered meat from the processor arrives at the pet food factory, it is ground and cooked and textured. Into the mix go salt, broth, preservatives, and various substances that serve as stabilizers. (These have their own histories of production which we will skip.) The result is a meat batter, wet and homogenous looking, made mainly of water, animal protein and fat. Think of this as a homogenous and generic paste, even if it is (sometimes) produced from single stream animal types (chicken, beef, salmon and so on). This fluid substance is heated in combination with a protein gel. The giant mixers do their work again blending gelling agents that might include crystalline forms of cellulose, dried milk, and egg whites as binders or a substance like bovine serum albumin, another highly processed animal by product. At this stage, before coloring and flavoring, the paste is considered "a multi-component gel" whose properties are generally described by their organic chemical structure. Vegetable agents are often used, guar gum and carrageenan, starch from beans or other sources, to get the "paste" to the right consistency. The mixer works away until the paste is smooth.

Flavor gets added using broths from various animal sources, as well as salt and other flavoring, to increase palatability. The paste needs to taste good or the cats won't eat it and the whole process will have been in vain. Believe me. Sweeteners, for concentrated flavorings known as digests are also added. These, too, have their origin narrative, made from a combination of natural and chemical materials. Laced with sorbic acid or other preservatives, and anti-oxidants to prevent breakdown of the fats, and coloring to be sure the meat look is present, the paste is ready for shaping. The mixture gets sent through metal plates with differently shaped holes that create the sliced, chunked, or paté varieties of the food.

The grains in the cat food have their own story. Food fertilizer depends on nitrogen, which is plentiful in the air around us. But getting the nitrogen into a usable form was difficult before the first decade of the 20th century. Already mentioned, two German chemists–Fritz Haber and Carl Bosch—developed a method that could expand to an industrial scale. The Haber-Bosch process is largely unknown to most of the people who benefit from this invention, which includes more than half of the world's current population. Their discovery converted nitrogen in the atmosphere to fertilizer and is still the basis of synthetic processes that support global food production. Over the decades, the conversion processes have steadily improved along with recycling of gasses and byproducts. Haber's work earned him a Nobel prize in 1918, but he was also responsible for weaponizing chlorine and other toxic gases that were used in World War I and is thus considered a pioneer in the dubious realm of chemical warfare. Off-gassing is hardly the term for such deliberate and instrumental outcomes. The contradiction of making a major contribution to the food supply while finding ways to destroy human lives at a massive scale is evident.

Now, at last, the food is ready to be canned. Before the cans are filled, they are sterilized, heated to about 120 degrees Centigrade for a little more than an hour, after which they are quickly cooled, both energy consuming operations. After filling, the cans are vacuum sealed, a highly industrial process, and their pull-tops applied. Vacuum sealing involves another system of specialized equipment capable of pulling the air from the can under heat and pressure at a high volume of production. Various heads and crimping rollers, rotation devices and pressure cams all participate in the process. A vacuum pump and stabilizer work in a sealed chamber to be sure the round metal cans are properly closed. Phew. Somewhere along the way, the pop-top was formed and attached, but I guess I wasn't paying attention... Now to the labels.

The label: Dressing it up
The label on the morning's can shows a photographic image of a cat, paw extended towards images of salmon steak floating in the air. Carefully cut out, the cat's face and whiskers are endearing and appealing, and of course, look away from us with appropriate feline interest in food and disinterest in human approval. The

images of food and cat were initially created in a studio, well-lit, and professionally produced. Did the cat come through a pet talent agency? Have an agent, a manager, a handler? Who set the lights and managed the photo shoot? How many hours, assistants, and accessories were required? Once the photos were taken, they had to be reviewed and vetted. Who made the selection of this particular image? What were they paid and where are they in the company hierarchy? Then the photo sent through a designer's toolkit to make prototype labels whose appeal is tested in marketing and focus groups. Is a black cat too off-putting? A white cat too esoteric and elite? A long-haired cat too luxurious? Tuxedo cat or ocelot spotted breed more charming? Go for a brown tabby or an orange tabby? All of these decisions have to be weighed carefully so that the result is generic enough to appeal to a broad range of cat owners.

My brand is not composed of wild sources. It is not rabbit or duck, and it is not created from all natural ingredients, as if that were possible, nor is it an elite brand suggesting it was designed by the cats themselves from their ancestral experience of being predators in jungle and forest environments. Still, the labels communicate the brand and the brand involves a campaign of information that immediately signals to the buyer that this is cat food for their cat.

Part Two: Feeding the Cats 247

The color of the label backgrounds—orange, brown, red, blue, pinkish—is a code for chicken, grilled meat, beef, seafood, and salmon and so on—so that the range of options is evident. The label includes a long list of ingredients, a waving banner with the flavor and the logo of the company, and phone number for customer service. A bar code for scanning at the check-out counter is printed on each label, and here another whole infrastructure system appears.

Bar codes are part of the interwoven connections of prices and price codes, of supermarket machines that read the codes. These are entered into each supermarket system independently, made consistent with the price point determined by the volume and rate at which these cans are consumed. The electronics in the scanner, its lights and beeps, sounds and customer rewarding haptic features are all activated by that little bar code. I can feel the satisfaction of the swipe and the deposit of the can in the bagging area. The ergonomics of the self-check station, or of the check-out line with a live assistant, are all engineered for the supermarket industry, their stainless steel surfaces aimed at a middle height. Who determines the right dimensions for these machines, the conveyor belts of the check-out apparatus with its guard rails and bumpers? And where are these made? And who designed the innards of the bar code reader? And the data systems to which they are connected? Their design and implementation came from where and when and was controlled by whom? And how often do these scanners and belts break down and get replaced and where does that waste go and how if at all is it recycled? And at what cost?

Ok. That is all too much to deal with. Back to the label on the can.

The labels have to be printed, cut, wrapped around the cans in another automated process. The inks on the labels and machines for printing, for processing the photo-lithographic plates, putting them onto high speed presses, with pigments extracted from all kinds of sources around the world, with varnish added at the end, are created from what? We tracked carbon black for the printed decal on my coffee mug, but skipped the details of the rest of printing ink. The paper on which the labels are printed comes from some source. Recycled paper or fresh forest material? Processed where? We are back to chemicals and stench flowing into the atmosphere, water waste runoff smelling from the process and racing downstream even after passing through various filtration beds and other cleansing procedures. The adhesives are a highly regulated substance. Any food substance packaging is not supposed to give off VOCs. In fact, the FDA has an entire set of guidelines for food and beverage packaging adhesives for attaching the label that are compliant with its rules. And that exists in a booklet, which can be ordered in print or downloaded as an e-book, its own brightly covered cover and printed pages another element in this unending chain. But the types and variety of labelling adhesives are many, and specific to the materials in the label as well as the kind of surface to which it will be adhered. Water based and hot-melt made of starch, casein (milk substances), or synthetic polymers. The details never end, and the mere fact of the label's being adhered to the can links it to industries and processes with their own lifecycle of waste and pollution, as usual.

The cans are marketed in groups, in boxes. These boxes, also have printed labels, their dimensions precisely manufactured to specifications, from more wood pulp and recycled materials, also processed with water, heat, chemicals and sent through a massive number of vats, machines, rollers, and presses before being scored and cut, folded and assembled with adhesives. And the source of the adhesives? Finally the whole package is shrink-wrapped in plastic for shipping. Or not.

Enough about the cat food and its packaging. Now to the cat food bowls, spoon, and the washing up.

● ●

250 AFFLUVIA

The bowls: Enduring pyrex
The clear strong pyrex bowls from which the cats eat and drink have lasted many years. A few bits of last night's meal stick to their surfaces, minute debris too small even for feline appetites. They ignore what has no interest, and

can't be bothered to lick the bowls clean. They, too, live within a margin of affluence.

The bowls are the outcome of industrial activities whose long history reaches back into Mesopotamia, as we saw looking at the glass jar for beans. As already discussed, humans figured out, probably by accident, that sand heated to a certain temperature turns into a hard brittle substance that has properties of endurance and resistance.[91] But we have also invented ways to use other materials that contain silicon, like quartz.

Glass is not reactive, and neither is pyrex, an "improved" glass product created in the early 20th century by the Corning corporation. Pyrex, like the glass discussed earlier, is made from silicon mixed with boric oxide. The mixture is heated to a super-high temperature which, apparently, loosens the molecules from their crystalline structure (chemicals go wild) and then fixes them in place in the cooling process before they can realign (they remain unruly). The alluring strangeness of glass inheres in this structure for which the technical term is an "amorphous solid."

Boric oxide and silicon are both essential components of glass, and we covered silicon mining earlier in terms of sand as a source. But quartz, one of the more common minerals on the surface of the earth, can also be a source for silica crystals. Quartz fields are found in the US in Arkansas and Oklahoma, in counties with names like

Pike, Pope, Hot Spring, Garland, Saline and Yell, named for settler figures, early politicians, and features of the landscape. Near the site in Arkansas, the Plum Bayou people once made quartz arrowheads and knives. Now called Toltec Mounds Park, it was a site of native settlement between about 650 and 1000 CE. It contains evidence of copper from Michigan and conch shells from the Gulf of Mexico, telltale signs of trade across a considerable region, as well as quartz artefacts. Now only three Toltec Mounds remain where it is believed eighteen once stood. These mounds were used in part for time-telling, to help with planning agricultural cycles and producing a predictable harvest. The Plum Bayou people abandoned the site, but the quartz in the region remained for later groups of indigenous people and then settlers.

The quartz crystals which make the Arkansas site so valuable are formed when silica (silicon dioxide) is heated. Between 280 and 245 million years ago, relatively recently in geologic time, heated underground water flowed through fissures and cracks in the region of the Ouachita Mountains. As the hot substance cools, each single silicon atom takes four oxygen atoms as its partners, bonding the selected family into a six-sided prism like a molecular square dance configuration. In addition to being beaten to pulverized dust to make sand for glass, quartz is used to regulate time in watches and clocks. When electric current goes through the crystal,

Part Two: Feeding the Cats   253

it vibrates at a high frequency (imagine, more than 32,000 times a second). This steady, tuning-fork like oscillation can be used to convert voltage into regular mechanical activity. I have no idea how. In addition to being used in time pieces—watches and clocks—quartz crystals are present in computers and sonar equipment to create mechanical accuracy.

But for glass production the quartz is pulverized (industrial machines), then heated with oxides from borax to add strength and durability to the glass. Borax is a white powder that was hauled out of the mining sites with teams of twenty mules, with one of the largest in Boron, California, starting in the 19th century. Borax is used as a cleaning agent as well as in many industrial manufacturing processes. The first borosilicates were used in lantern glass, replacing lenses that had been prone to shatter from the heat of kerosene flames. This is another product those Corning Glass works scientists invented. By 1912, they had discovered the properties of this material and blended it into a stable standard known as Pyrex.

Now this kind of glass is made in enormous quantities, large batches of raw materials mixed and heated to over 2,912o F and kept at that high temperature for up to 24 hours to rid it of bubbles that weaken its structure. The glass is molten, and flows toward the end of a tank with the thick deliberateness of syrup and before being sent through machines that form it into shapes by blowing and pressing, pulling and rolling, according to specific patterns. Some glass is shaped by air pressing it between two sides of a mold. Another process draws glass out so it can become a hollow tube, with air sent through its empty cavity until it becomes rigid and cool.

So the smooth clear bowls, now holding the wet food for the morning, chunked into pieces and placed on the floor, had their own history before arrival in my kitchen. From what ancient sites the quartz was taken and from which borax mines the materials were hauled is no longer evident. I cannot recover the sources of the materials any more than the destinations of the gasses that escaped in the process of their manufacture. Air pollution from the production of glass creates acid rain filled with nitrates, chlorine, and sulfates. Only some of this can be mitigated by precipitating elements from the smoke and vapor. This off-gassing has sometimes caused the State of New York to sue the Environmental Protection Agency to try to get enforcement of regulations to control emissions from the Corning Glass Works, where, as already noted Pyrex originated.

Now, it so happens that the countertop on which I set the half-empty cat-food can is made from quartz mining waste. The polished white composite glitters with bits of crystal, a sleek synthetic alternative to marble and granite. Sounds like a positive way to transform waste into useful products, neat and clean. But the process begins with pulverization, a

Part Two: Feeding the Cats 255

monstrous beating that turns hard rock into small bits, then combines it with all kinds of plastic resins whose sources, as we have seen, depend on mining, manufacturing, and waste. Pigments that are added also produce waste in their production, and some toxins. The newly mixed composite of quartz chips and synthetics is baked in an industrial oven, itself made of metal, fired with gas, and containing its own elaborate machinery. Who guards this yawning furnace, goads the material along the conveyors, watches to be sure nothing goes amiss along the way? The resulting countertop is non-porous, like the pyrex bowls, and also very durable. Because it is not reactive or absorptive, it poses fewer health risks than organic surfaces like wood or stone. Where nothing sinks in, nothing can be released. Anything released from the countertop into the atmosphere comes directly from the food, cleaning products, or other substances, as when I pass the smooth yellow side of the scrubby sponge over the surface to wipe away a few drops of liquid from the cat food can. The droplets of water that bead on the surface will soon evaporate, carrying with them whatever aromatics and volatiles that can become airborne.

We breathe about 23,000 times a day, and thus deal with about 130 cubic meters of air, and our nostrils take in odorous molecules that get stuck in the cilia and mucous of the nasal cavity and trigger responses in the olfactory nerve. Transmitted to the brain these signals produce a "sense" of smell. More gas. More airborne material. And no mention at all so far has been made of the costs of the mining processes, the raw extraction of substances and materials, the effects on the human beings who run the machines, work the sites, filter that air–or of the workers regulating the furnaces that heat the silica and boric mixture to the melting point and keep it there—or supervise the countertop material production. Who breathes what when along the way so that my cats have sturdy durable bowls for the wet food from their freshly opened can and a smooth countertop on which to wait?

Just by opening the can of food, I have participated in strip mining of bauxite ore someplace in the world, in the use of water, energy, and chemicals in a manufacturing process that is sustained with equipment whose design and manufacture I have not even factored into this narrative. I have been connected to mining and to the gruesome character of meat processing. The business of each of these is also connected to human supply chains, products, processes of banking, loans, cost-benefit analyses and all kinds of other systems of daily work, office labor, inventory control, and many other activities I have not taken into account. In addition, there are the buildings, the facilities, the trucks, the roads, the tires on the trucks and the workings of their engines, the electronics for tracking the shipments, and the equipment to load and offload the raw and finished materials, packaging and end products, each of which requires its own specialized skills and materials.

● ●

Part Two: Feeding the Cats   257

The Cheap Spoon: Cut and pressed
I use a small spoon, cheaply made, die cut from a sheet of metal alloy, to scoop the cat food from the can. The shape has ancient roots, the handle and bowl combinations of spoons are considered the oldest human utensil.

But shells and gourds and other natural objects served as spoons before the metal ones. Now this inconspicuous object shines with the polish of chrome, nickel, and steel. We've already been through enough descriptions of the production of aluminum and steel to know how it is made. Now picture the shining roll of metal alloy sliding across a bed on which a die cutter stamps out blanks. These flat silhouettes pass through rollers and then get trimmed. The shape emerges more precisely than before, a little thicker where the handle bending will occur. The image of Uri Geller, the Israeli telepath, who in the 1970s claimed to be able to bend spoons with the sheer force of his mind, rises as an immediate association. No real proof of his skills ever materialized (actually, the contrary, they were shown to be magic tricks) but he fascinated a generation with his claims of telekinetic ability.

The flat blanks are rolled, their shiny shapes catching light as they move toward the annealing ovens whose treatment will help prevent cracking under stress. The spoons are bent before they go into the intense heat, where the carefully controlled temperatures will make them strong, resistant to casual damage. Perhaps that was the problem for poor Uri, over-heated spoons, too excited to give in to his suggestions. The spoons emerge from their ovens and are carried along to the trimmers and pressers. There they get a scrape to become the perfect size before the final step when they slide into a fitted slot and are held firmly while two steel dies, harder than they are, make stamped impressions from

Part Two: Feeding the Cats

both back and front. The pattern appears in the handle, a combination of raised and depressed dots and curves, in imitation of those worked decorations of silver smiths whose craftsmanship created elegantly wrought organic lines and geometric shapes.

The stuff left over the from the cheap spoon production can be re-melted, returned to the huge mass from which it was separated into sheets, rolled, pressed for cutting, as was the case with the steel grinder blade. Metal working is about 8000 years old, though gold was worked much earlier since the soft and shiny metal was malleable as well as valuable and enduring. Then copper was used beginning around 4200 BCE, to make tools including weapons and implements. The "bronze age" begins in around 3300 BCE, and followed the era of copper by the discovery that additions of tin would strengthen the metal. But the cheap little spoon is made of some cheap alloy of steel, whose history we have already traced.

Back at the factory from which the spoon has issued, now packaged, shrink-wrapped, mounted on palettes and forklifted to a loading dock before being set onto a truck, the solid waste from its production produces slag, waste, and sludge. Once known as waste, it is now called by-product to emphasize the extent to which it can be channeled into reuse. These by-products are responsible for a host of health issues and also cause what is politely referred to as "degradation" of the environment. The language does not conceal the reality. The scale and frequency of these cycles is overwhelming.

Diagram 14: Natural gas

Natural gas is pumped from the ground source, processed in a plant where it is purified, processed, and stored. Supplies are often stored underground in caverns or empty extraction sites. Then it is piped to storage facilities near distribution sites where it is kept under high pressure until it is needed for homes, institutions, and industries.

Part Two: Feeding the Cats

Warmth: (Un)natural gas

As we shift attention to natural gas, water, waste, and electricity, we shift from examining the production of things to the creation of elaborate systems and processes linked to natural resources and their management.

The spoon, which now is dirty and needs washing, slips into the sink. The simple action of washing up will connect me with another geographically distributed but connected system of infrastructure deep in the earth and far from where they end up in my kitchen.

As I turn on the water tap the thermostat on the tank-less gas water heater sends a signal through the system. Gas, piped in and clean, burns blue and warm red-gold in flame to heat the water in the on-demand tank. The gas comes into the house because of the engineering of pressure differentials all along its route. Gas flows from high pressure to lower, and the distribution of natural gas makes use of this principle to gather, process, and deliver gas.

To be readily available to consumers, natural gas supplies are stored in depleted oil or gas fields, natural reservoirs from which the resources have been extracted. These underground sites are millions of years old and can be as deep as 5000 feet, almost a mile below the surface of the earth. Ancient beds of fossil fuels, empty and subterranean, are used for storage so the gas can be extracted in winter, replaced in summer when demand is lower, kept secure in the porous earth where it is kept under pressure simply by natural forces. Alternatively, the gas can be kept in fields of aquifers, water bearing rocks or empty salt caverns where it serves to supply gas for peak delivery demands short term.

From the earth and back to the earth, removed, purified, processed and then stored, the gas is the very essence of the earth's life cycles turned into a steady stream of fuel to supply heat and energy. And from the natural gas fields in, for instance, Texas, Louisiana, Pennsylvania, and Arkansas, methane leaks constantly. Tens of thousands of pounds of methane per hour is leaked into the atmosphere, which, astonishingly, is less than 1% of what is being produced. (In the United States, cattle supposedly produce a little more than 30% of all methane.) Affluvia. But the rate for natural gas is considered well within federal limits. The scientists who determined this number flew in a NOAA research aircraft to test air and estimate the distribution of leaks and other chemicals that are emitted as gas is produced. Many of these airborne pollutants contribute to regional issues of air quality and then seep into the ground and water.

One of the more astounding natural gas sites is a gaping crater known as the "Door to Hell" in Turkmenistan. This collapsed natural gas field was set on fire in 1971 to keep the toxic methane gas from going into the atmosphere. But the geologists miscalculated and the crater has been on fire ever since—more than half a century of burning because of human error. The Soviet engineers who started drilling the site for oil realized too late that it was natural gas in the field and the drilling rig collapsed into the subterranean cavern. Turkmenistan, which has almost no tourist industry, uses the site as an attraction even as it remains largely unregulated and dangerous to the curious who approach the burning pit.

The pipeline that arrives at my house begins at the wells where a gathering system makes use of compressors in the field. The internal combustion engines used to create pressure for transmission cannibalize their own gas as source fuel. As it comes from the well the gas contains some impurities that must be purged—the theme of purity prevails in processing. Various components like propane and butane that appear in the gas can be sequestered, siphoned off and used separately, sent through their own pipelines and slotted into production lifecycles until they end up in tanks, containers, and are consumed as flame or evaporate into the air as solvents. Helium, the laughing gas, is one of the impurities sometimes purged from natural gas, as are corrosives like sulfur. Each of these has a use and a destination far upstream from my water heater's gas supply. Does the gas remember its ancestral cousins, even as it flows, purified and productive, into its final state as combustion? Does it giggle along the way while the helium is still present? Unlikely.

How far did the gas travel to my house, to the outdoor cabinet where the just-in-time heater sits in a ventilated space? More than 250,000 miles of steel pipe exist in the national transmission system, though the gas flowing into my heater may have only travelled a fraction of that distance, not much farther than a kid on a cross-country road trip. Most of the natural gas in Los Angeles comes from out of state, but how far? A map linked to SoCal Gas shows transmission lines from near Lancaster, Palmdale, and other points north and east. But the place where gas is taken from the ground is not clear.

The number of stops on the route from production to local distribution means the gas does not move as a crow flies, but rather is subject to the kinks and joints of a transportation system. All along the way, the gas is under pressure, serious pressure, from 200 to 1,500 pounds per square inch. Compare this to the seventy pounds per square inch that the human jaw can exert with the back molars. In populated areas in particular, the pipelines cannot approach their pressure limits (for safety reasons) so the transmission slows down. To maintain smooth delivery, redundancy is built into the system. Parallel lines move the gas along without interruption, and at regular intervals, while compressors increase the pressure to keep it flowing.[92]

Automation exists within this elaborate system, and so feedback loops and multiple systems for communicating from the pipeline to a control room also exist, built so that the shut off valves can be operated remotely along the lines. The speed of flow is about the legal limit of a tractor, in the 30 mile an hour range, so the gas would have

Part Two: Feeding the Cats

a leisurely transit from the Texas oil fields to remote destinations. Everything is monitored: pressure, flow, demand, routes and travel times and when the gas arrives at a local utility company. The pressure is modified again locally to make it appropriate for consumer use in terms of rate of flow and, interestingly, odor. At this point affluvia is manufactured deliberately, as an odorant is added that makes gas detectable in even very small amounts. The smell of natural gas is in fact unnatural.

The pressure drops along the route taken by the gas. Dribbling through the pipeline, it arrives in smaller and smaller pipes until it flows into the connection to the house. The number of safety features built into the system insures that regulators and relief valves can operate automatically, but these, too, are designed to exhale gas into the atmosphere if and when a contingency arises that requires it. Linked as I am to a service line from a utility, I also have the required residential meter where, as the gas industry itself suggests, the pressure has become less than that "created by a child blowing bubbles through a straw in a glass of milk." This image of innocence belies the complexity of the system, of course, making it appear familiar and normal. But this is the process by which, subtle and well-regulated, the gas pressure in the system remains ever so slightly higher than the air pressure allowing it to flow out into the appliances and ignite with a spark from the pilot light. This account of natural gas is just the back story for simply turning on the hot water for a moment to rinse the spoon from the cat food.

Laborers in the natural gas industry often work far more than the forty-hour week for which they are paid as salaried employees. Violations of the Fair Labor Standards Act are rarely brought to attention under US law even though various law firms have identified themselves as specialists in such compensation cases. Risks to workers in the industry, amazingly, are mainly from traffic fatalities, exhausted drivers transporting workers to and from the fields. But the list of potential on-the-job hazards created by OSHA contains a staggering number of possible injury-causing accidents: being crushed by equipment, burnt by sudden ignition of leaks of flammable gases from mobile engines and auxiliary motors, or even being shocked by static electricity built up in a plastic pipe. Falling, being stuck in confined spaces, and working with aged or corroded fittings in a high-pressure supply line all fall under OSHA's list of potential hazards for workers in the industry.

The simple act of turning on the hot water tap at my sink to rinse the spoon which I have used to scoop the cat food connects me to this natural gas pipeline and workers all along the way. Now, what about the water?

Water: The long journey
Transparent and fluid, the water streams from my kitchen tap as I fill my coffee maker, rinse the cat food can, and wipe the counter with a moist sponge. Water. So miraculous I can hardly imagine its creation. Where did it come

Part Two: Feeding the Cats 267

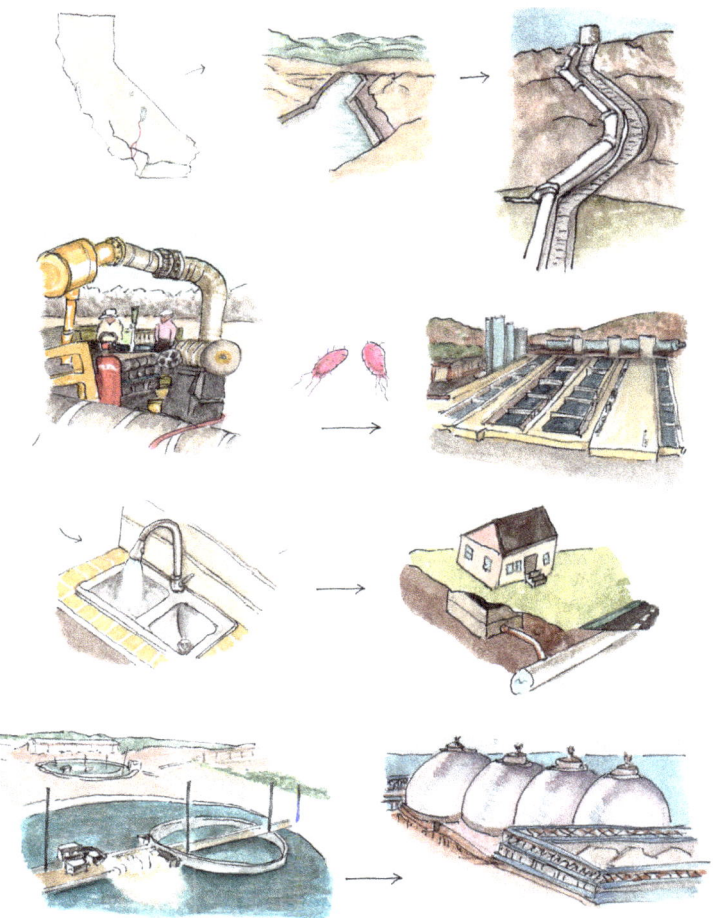

Diagram 15: Water and waste

Water from various sources is directed through an elaborate system of aqueducts and pipelines using the force of gravity as an aid in moving it across vast distances. Put under pressure and into pipes, it arrives at a treatment plant before being delivered to homes and businesses. The waste water moves into the municipal sewer system and is sent to a waste processing plant. Some of the water is stored for reuse and some is released.

from, this beautiful clear liquid with its agile motion and unscripted actions? How is it I can even see this amazing substance, know it is there, as it twists and splashes in the air between the faucet and the sink before disappearing down the drain. Even eschewing the cosmic context and origin stories in the Big Bang from which hydrogen emerged, which might be stretching our tale, the story of the water I use daily still spins out along many lines of geological history and current events.

The source: Ongoing conflicts
The total volume of water on Earth stays the same. Not only is it hard to make, but we can't make it. At any given time, it could be in a liquid, gaseous, or solid state. But with the exception of additional water from meteorites, the amount remains the same.

Oddly, water is both abundant and scarce. Fresh water is only a small portion of the total water on earth, as most water is in the salty oceans. The majority of fresh water exists as frozen ice, and the rest as streams, lakes, rivers and groundwater (which is mostly hidden underground). And drinking water is only 1% of the total so access to clean water is possibly the single most significant factor in human health and well-being, along with clean air.

Water has unique properties. Science blogs provide amazing facts about water's boiling point and freezing temperatures.[93] Water stays liquid at far higher temperatures than expected for reasons that have to do with the structure of this tiny molecule. The triangular structure consists of two hydrogen atoms and one oxygen atom.[94] Oxygen is the charismatic member of the trio, and the hydrogen side becomes more positive because its electrons are flirting with the oxygen, hanging out in its orbit. (Subatomic romance.) Hydrogen was the primal atom, the first formed in the universe, with its single proton and electron, and of course those mythic entities are not the little billiard balls of your childhood science project, but merely forms of energy configured according to regular rules of atomic structure. When the water freezes, these positive and negative sides get into a fixed configuration and thus make a solid, while in their liquid state they are in motion.

This is getting far too granular for making coffee or washing a spoon, but something about contemplating the fantastic cosmological origins of basic substances inspires a profound awe that infuses the morning routine with wonder.

Our water, the water in my tap, comes either from ground water or surface water (rivers, lakes, run-off). Much of the contemporary California landscape has been radically changed by dams, aqueducts, canals, and levees and systems for shifting water resources from the wetter northern part of the state to the central valley and southern part of the state. The water wars in California have a long history including complex negotiations among constantly competing interests. In essence, I am drinking the outcome of conflict. In California, agriculture absorbs more than 60% of water, with urban use at about 16%. Groundwater and wells are an enormous source of water, more than 85% of Californians depending on it for drinking water. But drinking water is a deceptive phrase. The same water that runs through my tap and into my coffee canister is used for my shower and toilet and washing machine. I might as well be using chardonnay to flush…

In Los Angeles, we get our water from a combination of sources, the California Aqueduct, The Colorado River Aqueduct, and the State Water Project. These names only hint at the distances between sources and tap, and what happens along the way. The beautiful Owens valley is on the eastern side of the Sierras, some of the most dramatic landscape in the state. How this came about is a tale of intrigue and deal-making, but in 1905, the city of Los Angeles managed to secure water rights to the river and lake in this valley.[95] We then built an aqueduct, completed in 1913, that goes for about 250 miles. At the time, it channeled four times as much water as the city needed. But that was in 1913. Farmers in the Owens Valley, forced to stop doing water-intensive crop raising and replace it with cattle grazing, dynamited the aqueduct, but did not prevail. It was rebuilt.

Water treatment: From sky to sink
Water was also a major source of disease before mass treatment plants were put in place. Typhoid and cholera,

Part Two: Feeding the Cats

two huge killers, had to be identified and then eliminated.

But besides microorganisms, other toxins also get into the water along its path. Imagine, rainwater or ice melt filtering its way through the multiple layers of rock between the surface and a water table. Sulfur, zinc, arsenic are all naturally occurring substances, and they get picked up along the way. In addition, fertilizers, mine waste, and industrial water run off get into the drainage systems. Even pure rain water gets polluted with minerals, some toxic, by-products of industry, and then, septic seepage of various kinds. And if one is in an urban area, the street runoff carries gasoline and motor oil while yards and golf-courses add their share of toxins in the form of pesticides. Nice. Yummy even. The clear clean liquid becomes a hot mess. And it also stinks and tastes bad.

So the companies—private and public—that process the water have to treat it for all of these things and make the nasty substance back into the liquid that appears from my tap. They want to be sure that the water has a nice clarity, good taste and smell, isn't cloudy or discolored from any weird pollutants or flourishing colonies of microorganisms, and, in addition, that it isn't too acid, too base, or too anything else. Finally, just to please the conspiracy theorists, fluoride is added to the water to prevent (believe it or not) tooth decay. Partisans fall on all sides of that decision, with some determined to believe this dosing of the water supply creates its own effects and mind controls to those who believe that it was tooth decay itself that was part of a plot launched by an evil mind and their far-reaching empire. After all, the first law regulating water in the United States was the Quarantine Act which in 1893 was passed to keep out foreign contaminants. Nice symbolism.

In the course of the 20th century, water regulations paid attention to an increasing range of issues. The earliest regulations were aimed at the poor little microorganisms and attempts to eliminate their influence by using chlorine to do them in. The elimination of heavy metals—zinc, copper, lead—came next, just at the beginning of WWII, in 1941. In California, standards for water were only passed in the early 1960s. The Federal Safe Drinking Water Act of 1974 gives the Environmental Protection Agency the authority to test water everywhere in the United States, but increasingly, they deal with the unintended consequences of the purification process itself since the chlorine involved has a tendency to interact with other substances.

But let's start at the beginning of my water's journey. Imagine you are a little modest water molecule, maybe part of a cloud in a volatile atmospheric situation. You fall from the sky in the Sierras and freeze as part of a snowfall and get packed down into a solid mass. As the season tilts and the air heats up you feel yourself disengaging from your companions, able to move more freely and tumble downhill as part of a spring runoff. You join a little freshet, which feeds into a stream and you have the ride of a lifetime in a fast-moving current over smooth rocks along a lively course. You flow past Bishop and Big Pine, located against the dramatic backdrop of the Eastern side of the Sierras. You can sense the crashing waters, the force of energy carving away the bank in the rush, but you hurtle along as the stream joins others and becomes a river flowing into a lake in the Owens Valley. Here the sky is reflected in your water and the brilliant sun and clouds fill up the view. You might pause in the long ago once flourishing Tinemuha and Haiwec Reservoirs, or get the smallest glimpse of the final puddles that remain of the Owens Lake, once a regular refuge for massive flocks of migrating birds. Now dust control is a major issue in the Valley and water has to be diverted back to dampen the dry lake bed enough to keep the air quality from being dangerous to residents. But your course is ever onward.

The river narrows and you are sucked into a dark intake, a culvert that punctures a concrete embankment in the river bank. Now you are in the system, drawn into a downward tumble from this high valley to the distant world of Los Angeles nearly four thousand feet lower. You can hear the crank and whirr of machinery opening the diversion gates that control the flow. For a few minutes, your path is blocked. You pool in a momentary backwash against the closed sluice and then it opens. You race through a concrete conduit with special hydraulic design features including heavy duty sealant. Once again you are in free rapid motion, caught in the momentum of the stream. You are following a path laid down more than a hundred years ago, when the machinations of William Mulholland, Richard Eaton, and Joseph Lippincott (connected with the Owens Valley water deal mentioned above) conspired to grab land and water rights from the region to supply the growing needs of the rapidly expanding city of Los Angeles. Your path is part of a questionable historical past that is now baked into the infrastructure of the area.

Lined canals and covered conduits guide your path until you are shunted into either an open trough or a pipeline that shoots over the hills and valleys until you come careening down the Cascades section of the aqueduct at full tilt. The elegant structure is now a historical landmark in recognition of its engineering. At the top of the Cascades an enormous concrete holding tank is the final resting point of water that has come across hundreds of miles of concrete pathways. The labor, excavation, construction, and materials involved are greater than that required for an interstate or railroad, and perversely, the town built for temporary housing of personnel working on the Second LA Aqueduct was named Shangri-La Estates.[96]

You could be a molecule from another source, like groundwater or the Colorado River Aqueduct, since about half of Los Angeles's water comes from the latter. This aqueduct begins at the California-Arizona border and consists of tunnels, canals, conduits, siphons and pumping stations.

Part Two: Feeding the Cats

It is considered one of the Seven Modern Engineering Wonders by the American Society of Civil Engineers. The water runs through the desert, often in open canals, and has to be pumped up over Parker Dam in a process that consumes massive amounts of electricity generated by Hoover Dam. Phew.

Three possible sources—the Colorado River Aqueduct coming from the East, the Los Angeles Aqueduct from the Northeast, and the State Water Project bring water from the Delta in the Bay Area. In addition, storm water, groundwater, and various streams of recycled water contribute to the total supply. The Aqueduct Filtration Plant can treat up to 600 million gallons of water a day.[97] In cryptic language, its home page describes improvements that include replacing the "existing cryogenic oxygen plant" with a "pressure swing adsorption plant" that can use "molecular sieve technology." Photos of the plant show various facets of the treatment and one particularly engaging image of a group of workers releasing hundreds and hundreds of "shade balls" to cover the reservoir. The webpage says they have 96 million of these, all made from high density polyethylene, and use them to protect from sunlight-triggered activity in the water.

Massive reservoirs exist for storage. But open-air storage is no longer viable because the water gets polluted, the molecules combine with cancer-causing chemicals. So, little molecule, after all of that travel along open and closed aqueduct lines, through pipes and down the cascades, shaken up and even weary you arrive at a holding pool that is covered so you cannot get into trouble with the air. Dark and somber, the reservoir is the last stop before you are sucked into a water treatment facility where various strange things take place. First you are subject to coagulation and flocculation.[98] Sounds a little kinky, but these processes bond chemicals to any dirt or particles that are in the water and this causes the formation of *floc*. Then the floc settles out, being heavy, and leaves you floating freely above with your clean companions. Well, almost clean. You still pass through a mess of filters, mainly sand, gravel, and charcoal, so that any remaining dirt is removed, but also, any parasites, bacteria, and other organisms that have floated along with you and are hanging out among the water molecules. Just in case that isn't enough, you and your companions are dosed with chlorine (or chloramine) to get rid of any remaining living beasties. Some municipalities also give the water a boost with additives to its chemical composition, making it harder, softer, less likely to corrode pipes.[99]

The photographs of the water treatment plants show vast pools and a fretwork of steel girders, pipes, and pumps. Once again, we are in the land of industrial processes. Huge tanks and fittings, elaborate ladders, walkways, valves, and controls. Details on the production and manufacture of all of this? Too much to address, but just glance at online images, imagine what is required to produce every aspect of this elaborate infrastructure. Metal—extracted, processed, formed, cast, transported, assembled, treated for weather resistance—is combined with electrical power to move the water through the system as it is purified and treated to conform to regulatory standards.

In Southern California, we do not have a major legacy of lead pipe in homes, but lead piping is still part of the service lines that deliver water. In the home, the hazard that is largely avoidable, except in much older homes. To get the water from the treatment plant to the house, pumps are essential though water pressure can be generated by storing the liquid in an elevated tank. New York city apartment buildings are famously dotted with these rooftop water towers, as ancient as the buildings on which they perch, wood slatted or metal structures.

At domestic residences, like my house, the connection to the water main is crucial.[100] Water is pumped from the reservoir at the filtration plant into the public utility system. A "lateral line" connects the main to each house. Somewhere, near the intake valve and shut-off with which I am familiar, a regulator must be working to keep the pressure stable and safe. But the basic pressure in the faucets in my single-story house comes from the force with which the water moves through the utility lines. The pressure is always there. I open the faucet and out comes the gush of fresh clear water through the tap. I don't have to create suction or operate a hand-pump or flip a switch, just turn the handle on the tap. Throughout my neighborhood, the city of Los

Angeles, the state, and most of the United States, these municipal supply lines have been put into place.

Permanent wells have been identified in human settlements as old as 6500 BCE, and in Neolithic Scotland, some indoor water systems with intake and waste removal date to about 3000 BCE. In Crete, buried clay water pipes created a delivery and sanitation system—with the remains of a flush toilet from about 1800 BCE, according to the field notes of archaeologists excavating the area. The Romans were famous for their water engineering, the Nepalese were equally expert, while Mayans and others in the Americas designed their own ingenious systems. But large-scale municipal water and sewage management systems, particularly in the increasingly dense urban areas of Europe and America, were mainly mid-to-late 19th century innovations. Contaminated water was deadly, and the need for sanitation became increasingly evident in cities like London, Paris, New York, Chicago, Hamburg, and elsewhere by the 19th century. Retrofitting cities with sewer systems was a non-trivial matter, and in a city like Los Angeles, where the growth of the population has been exponential, the infrastructure has a constant challenge to keeps up with development.

The water has come into the house. Little molecule, you have arrived in my kitchen. The stream runs clear and clean from my tap. But it needs to be a bit warm to wash the cat food cans and serving spoon. For that? Gas and

Part Two: Feeding the Cats

electricity are needed, as we saw in the earlier section on washing the spoon. We've cheated a bit on the water discussion, not really giving details on the various processes in the filtration plant, the chemicals, the screens, the sources of carbon filters, manufacture of every pipe and valve, and have said almost nothing about the labor involved.

Wastewater management is actually a profession, and degrees in water treatment technology exist to train and certify employees in the field. On the job training is also a part of the preparation, and licensing is required according to individual state regulations. Workers monitor the flows, direct the addition of chemicals, keep track of samples and testing, and generally have to be familiar with all aspects of the plant's operation as well as with emergency preparedness in the event of floods, earthquakes, or other disasters. Aside from the hazards of tripping, falling, or even drowning (it has happened) the workers have to monitor their own exposure to hazardous chemicals and biohazards.[101]

The affluvia is becoming apparent, and the off-gassing of water treatment creates problems that can be an issue in a worker's personal air zone. Foodborne, airborne, and fecal transferable bacteria are present in the water treatment plants, and protecting against infection is essential though OSHA has no standards for limits of exposure to many of these, including endotoxins that can cause Hepatitis A. Personal protective equipment of various kinds is recommended, including goggles, face shields, steel-toed boots that are removed on leaving the plant, and so on.[102] Tough to work with water.

• •

Waste: More expertise
I rinse the bits of remaining cat food off the metal spoon under the running tap water. Tiny bits of purplish-grey matter flush down the drain. I also empty the leftover coffee from yesterday, turning the pot almost upside down as the brown liquid pours through the black plastic spout. Down the drain and out of sight, the combined liquids of acidic substances, colorants, animal by-products, preservatives, and other materials are carried away. But not really. They find themselves contributing to the massive streams of sewage, the lower end of the consumption system, which now races towards its own destination.

Down the drain, around the loops and bends, the waste moves with gravity's aid into the downward path to the main sewer line. The connection to the house is buried under the yard. The inspection done at the time of purchase included having a video camera inserted into the line to see what state of open-or-clogged condition it was in—the equivalent of a sewer line colonoscopy. The video has all the drama of a spelunking expedition below a bathtub—in other words, none at all—and the blurred indistinct images meant nothing to me, though I kept the video for its novelty value.

Now I can only hope that the connection is open and the water continues to pass through the pipes. They are only seventy years old, not ancient by domestic standards, and in my yard, at least, I think not threatened by tree roots or other vegetable kingdom invasions, though one never knows, until it is too late, what underground progress towards strangulation is taking place.

By some course through the 6,700 miles of public sewers, the water will find its way to the Hyperion waste water treatment plant, a vast facility (the site is 200 acres) just south of Playa del Rey.[103] Its many covered tanks and elaborate infrastructures manage to keep a surprisingly low profile at the edge of the Pacific Ocean next to Dockweiler Beach—the same spot where raw sewage got dumped into the ocean until about a hundred years ago. Run by the LA Department of Public Works and Bureau of Sanitation, the plant runs constantly to purge the waste water of Los Angeles of its many organic and inorganic threats.[104] This is the collection point for everything that comes through the sewer lines. The language on the website of a consulting firm responsible for engineering its "digester expansion" is suggestive, filled with terms that describe de-watering, centrifuge expansion, and increases in sludge flows.[105] Imagine—sludge flows from the sewers of Los Angeles. What comes to mind? A thick brown-grey mud teeming with life and toxins…as for the "digester"….?

Unlike the filtration plant that purifies the water coming

into Los Angeles through the aqueducts, this plant deals with water that has passed through the entire lifecycle of use and pollution going through the city. The wiki site claims it is the largest treatment plant west of the Mississippi River, and this seems hard to dispute.[106] Where else is a population so large an area so vast and an urban system so extensive as in metropolitan Los Angeles?

The Hyperion plant, again quoting the Wiki, was opened in 1950, but within a decade the volume of wastewater had increased past the point where treatment levels could be maintained. As they say, delicately, the engineers designed a five-mile pipe to dump "primary and secondary effluent" directly into the ocean. Nice. And while they had previously processed much of the waste into fertilizer, they opted instead to dump that into the ocean as well seven miles out. The sense that the ocean was so vast it could handle any amount of human waste was a prevailing myth in the 1950s. Marine life suffered and pretty soon the areas around the dumping sites had only worms and clams still living in them. Enough. You get the picture and it fulfills expectations of what sewage pollution does.

On average, the plant now processes 450 million gallons (1.7 billion liters) of sewage a day. The average American, just to get a sense, produces about 150 liters of waste water per day. With a population of about 10 million, the County of Los Angeles thus produces just about 1.5 billion liters of waste water, and that does not count the water from groundwater, industry, or businesses. The sludge flow is unimaginable, a constant landslide of waste…. The plant has its own power source that runs on methane it collects from the processing, and some of the water can be recycled back to irrigation or industry.

So, my cat food and coffee mixture runs through the encrusted interiors of underground sewer lines, gets to the plant after following a labyrinthine maze.[107] The water joins company with the flushed toilets, washing machine outlets, and shower drains and flows into the first part of the plant, the Headwater. Here the big things get taken out. "Bar screens" are metal grids that catch sticks, plastic bags, insect and rodent carcasses and other items that have managed to find their way into the moving stream.[108] The next step is for the water to go through a sedimentation tank where solids are removed—and driven to landfills. At that point, no particular anti-bacterial or cleaning procedures have occurred. Another round of sedimentation is part of what is known as the "primary" process. This takes place in enormous closed tanks that are kept shut to control odors as wastes are constantly removed from the surface of the liquid. Yummy.

Secondary treatments involved injecting bacteria into the waste water so it can be "denitrified" and "nitrified" as the bacteria feed and then rapidly decompose. An entire industry exists to supply bacteria for these purposes. One company, Bacteria Direct, provides a wide suite of products for every kind of task: algae control, aquaculture, animal feeding operations, food and beverage processors, industrial and chemical processors, petrochemical/hydrocarbon removal, biodiesel, pulp and paper, sludge reduction, and more![109]

Each of these areas is represented on its home page with a bright, light, sunny photograph of scenes with shining tanks, bright blue skies, or other cheerful sights. I click on the municipal treatment plant—a photograph of an open concrete pool reflecting a dark blue sky, its pure flat surface broken only by steel strut-work that is part of its operation. I find that the challenges for municipal and private plants are fats, oils, and greases (FOG) that have to be broken down. Fortunately, Bacteria Direct can supply Municipal DeFOG with bacteria that specifically target food processing waste. This product is described as a "tan, free-flowing powder with an earthy odor on a wheat bran/sodium sulfate carrier"—in other words, a dietary supplement for waste water that is laced with a blend of bacillus and "non-pathogenic Pseudomonas."[110] And if you want to calculate how much you need, just "compare the colony forming units per gram." Easy.

When I google the non-pathogenic Pseudomas I find elaborate cladistics to show their lineage and identity within a whole family of bacteria. Amazing. Probing further in the gallery of images, I am rewarded with translucent agar plates of cultures with characteristic patterns—the living cities of bacterial existence. Just a small glimpse of the rich literature on this species offers a view into agriculture, medicine, industry, and super-specialized research. The infinite granularity of expertise is amazing, and the sheer amount of material published on this one tiny topic to supply information across these multiple sectors of contemporary life gives some sense of how deep the underpinnings of Bacteria Direct would be if we probed further. Instead, take this tiny scratch in the surface of this knowledge base and we can go back to the next stage of the water treatment at Hyperion.

Having been treated with the bacteria, which are summarily "decomposed", the water has to have the "activated sludge" generated in that process settled out by sheer force of gravity. In other words, the water has to calm down, let the sludge settle and fall to the bottom. Some of this sludge goes back into the aeration tanks used for the first process, so a deep divide is made between RAS, returned activated sludge—and WAS (waste activated sludge) which is cast off. Hyperion apparently is pretty successful at recycling its sludge to keep the bacterial process going in the first process by sending the by-product from the second phase back to those tanks. Who designed all of this? Where are the controls in the plants? What do the valves and pumps look like? Who works there, managing the flows, monitoring sudden overflows or peak levels of bacterial activity?

Even with the sludge gone, the water still needs to be filtered further. For some reason, this requires diamond-shaped cloth filters. And just to be sure that the solids are removed, a chemical process is initiated in which a cationic polymer coagulates with any "colloidal-sized solids." You may be forgiven for not having a clue about what that means, what size those solids are, and which of any cationic polymers might be chosen for the task. Between Science Direct, letting me know that these are polymers that carry a positive charge, and Beckart Environmental, a major manufacturer of these polymers made specifically for wastewater treatment, I have many options. The company can sell you any of its existing product line or tailor specific solutions for your needs. Coagulants, filter aids, sludge conditioners—a whole host of products are available. How to choose?

As per most industry sites, this one contains an embedded video with a happy employee in a company shirt touring the industry operations. The company designs and engineers such items as "high-press filters" and the video is full of images of brightly colored plastic and metal machines, their parts moving in choreographed harmony, neatly clamped hoses, and computer screens with special-effects level diagrams. Everything works perfectly and the company guarantees it can help your business arrive at zero discharge levels. The positive tone, the euphemistic use of technical terms, and the reassuring rhetoric of the script all combine into a finely functioning bit of promotional

Part Two: Feeding the Cats 287

rhetoric. Peering into the images of the elaborate machinery and watching the operator flip switches on the accompanying "programmable logic controllers" provokes associations with nearly every dystopic futuristic film one has ever seen. Terry Gilliam's 1985 film *Brazil* is my common reference point for any scenario that includes ductwork, but Beckart is far from a destructive force, and the level of expertise on view in the company's public relations material is impressive.

Back to Hyperion where the water, now relieved of its solids, is about to be subject to yet another phase called "digestion." Disease-causing organisms remain in the biosolids, which have been pumped into enormous egg-shaped tanks called "digesters." These are closed environments, devoid of oxygen, where anaerobic bacteria are put to work. They work away in the dark for about two weeks, eating about half of the biosolids and destroying the pathogens. In the process, they release methane gas, which, again, becomes part of the whole energy cycle for the treatment plant. The remaining biosolids get centrifuged to remove excess water—think of a washing machine spin cycle—and they are offered to farmers. The City owns its own farm, Green Acres (no kidding), in Kern County and there it raises grain for livestock feed. Some of the biosolids get mixed with zoo waste and other materials for compost or non-food agriculture, the risk of disease being too great if it is used to grow plants for human consumption. [111]

So, now, I imagine that the water from my rinsed spoon

combined with cold coffee has snaked its way from my kitchen sink through the municipal water system and through the layers, coils, and torments of treatment to be thrust out into the ocean a few miles from shore while the last remains of whatever cat food and coffee grounds have been sucked, filtered, centrifuged and settled out of the liquid and are spending the next phase of their no-longer differentiated existence as biomass spread on a field to grow feed corn. Not a bad fate, in fact, to lie peacefully under the warm California sun and nurture another living being. They have given up their methane, obediently, in the process of being treated, but in the open air they continue to off-gas slowly, releasing their redolent contributions to the atmosphere.

• •

Electricity: The energy of electrons
All of everything seems to need electricity—the action of the coffee pot, the lights in my kitchen, thermostat in the water heater, and every step along the way of every process that is part of industrial manufacture from extraction to transportation, production and distribution and final operation. So I cannot very well skip a discussion of its production and transport to my home. But where is that electricity made? By what means? And how is it transported or conducted to the outlets in my house?

Do I even know what electricity *is* or how it works? In

my primitive understanding, I originally conceived of electricity as the movement of electrons through a conducting substance—as if individual particles were racing along a freeway of copper, bumping into each other and shuttling along. That is about as sophisticated as conjuring an image of an atom as a tinker-toy model of moving parts. Simply stated, this model is not true. But to explore how that is the case, we have to venture into the world of nuclear physics.[112]

Though the concept of atoms has been around in western science since the Greeks, the notion of vibrations as the core component of the universe has a longer history in Eastern philosophy. The vibrating energy theory of everything has come to be accepted by some physicists as providing a better explanation of natural phenomena like waves, gravity, magnetism, electricity, and the behavior of substances and materials than the older paradigms of discrete particles. But whether we subscribe to the vibratory energy or the tiny balls in motion model of the atom, the upshot is the same: electricity is the result of negative charges in motion. After all, the "particles" in an atom are merely positive and negative charges in motion. The moving negative charges get called electrons and they make up electricity. Precisely what a charge is, how it is bounded, contained, identified, measured, or defined is still a mystery to me.

As mentioned earlier in discussion of the coffee grinder motor, one of the major miracles of modern life was the taming of the motion of electrons towards human purposes and activities. Without electricity, modern life would not exist. Period. That simple. Steam power could not have mounted the level of production that electrical energy supports. But more profoundly, electricity was and is the core of telecommunication technology beginning with telegraph to telephone. And though optical fiber conducts light (hence its name) instead of electricity, all of the devices for input, storage, output, processing, and display of data are electricity dependent.

To be useful, electricity must be managed. We can't tame the static electricity that is generated mechanically by rubbing or by the build up on charges in a lighting storm. We can, however, manage what is called current electricity.[113] The movement of electrons shifting from one atom to another is electricity.[114] Exactly what this means is unclear, since it seems that it is the transfer of charge, not the actual movement of negatively charged particles, that produced electrical current. For sure, electrons are the wanton and errant citizens of the subatomic world, and their ability to move freely, jump out of their orbits, join other atoms or just go off on their own makes them volatile and destabilizing—but also, exciting in the physical as well as intellectual sense of that word.

Electricity cannot be mined or accessed as a direct resource, but has to be generated from a source of energy. Because of this, it is termed "secondary" energy. In the United States about 20% of electricity is generated from renewable sources (wind, hydro, solar, biomass, geothermal), almost the same amount from both coal and nuclear energy, and the rest from natural gas.[115]

Electrical current has direction and moves as a flow. Its power is an effect of the rate of flow of the charge (I am holding back from saying flow of electrons). To persuade the energy to move, a difference in charge has to be instigated between the start and end points of current. Electrical energy will go towards the positive charge in order to equalize the electric potential of a system. For electricity to move into a device in your home, you have to flip a switch that closes a circuit and that causes the electrical energy to flow.

Sounds easy. Except, of course, all of this depends on design and engineering features that are part of the municipal grid and your domestic wiring system with all of its insulation, circuit breakers, and fuses among other features.

In Los Angeles, the Department of Water and Power is in charge of supplying electricity to what is basically the largest utility system in the United States. It employs almost 10,000 people. The County has ten times that many employees (100,000). The urban electrical grid only emerged at the beginning of the 20th century, and it was about 1916 before the LADWP could distribute electricity. Sources for electrical power in Los

Angeles come from as far away as Oregon, Wyoming, and Utah.[116] First energy has to be generated at a power plant. That means a source of power needs to be nearby—water, wind, coal firing and so on. Then it passes through a "step up" transmission station then through a wide and interconnected network before passing through a "step down" substation into distribution networks, through transformers, and into the home.

This is another of the elaborate systems revealed by a glance into basic daily tasks and their simple-seeming operations. My simple flip of the switch connects me to vast areas of the western lands of the United States, to high dry rocky regions and powerful rivers as well as wind farms and fields of solar panels.

Power plants are the driving force of contemporary life and economy. They pump energy into the infrastructure. But the steps involved are many.

The "step up" substation is where the electrical current gets supercharged, its voltage intensified, so it can move to its destination with a minimal loss of power. The substation has the imposing look of a cross between a battleship and an over-sized car battery. Armored, metal, hooked up with pipes, wires, cables, and all kinds of heavy duty apparatus. What is it doing? What coils and mechanical devices are at work

Part Two: Feeding the Cats   293

to concentrate voltage to transmission lines and carry it hundreds of miles in insulted wires linked from one giant steel transmission tower to another? How much insulating material is needed to keep the electricity safely contained? Where does this transfer occur in underground circuits in areas of high urban density? My suburban Los Angeles home is fed by above-ground wires, which of course makes them vulnerable to wind, weather, falling trees and other hazards.

Once the electricity gets close to the city, it has to be "stepped down" in another substation that lowers the voltage enough to make it safe before it is split off for local distribution. How does the voltage get lowered? And then, nearby, even as close as the corner of my street, I can see the elaborate but oddly exposed and crude looking collection of transformers, resistors, and wires that then connect directly to my home. Its entrance and consumption is monitored by a meter, and the electricity come in through a box that is equipped with circuit breakers and fuses to mitigate against surges and unforeseen events.

This is, so far, a highly schematic and essentially uninformative tale. Go back a little in history. The first electric power plant was built by none other than the remarkable Thomas Edison.[117] This was in 1882, and what Edison realized was that simply burning fuel to make heat would not be sufficient to generate electrical energy—which had to be created from a turbine that powered a generator. The generator is the electricity making machine. This is similar to realizing that ice cream is not made from milk and ice, but from the action of a crank transforming the state of the ingredients into another form. But while ice cream flows mainly towards consumption, electricity can flow through the electrical grid to be itself transformative in its application. In terms of affluvia, however, note that more than 60% of most power generated from fossil fueled plants is wasted as heat.[118] Thermal pollution is not neutral or innocent.

At the power plant, fuel burned in a giant furnace releases heat which flows into a boiler to produce steam from cold water. The steam turns the blades of a turbine which generates kinetic energy. While the cooling towers take care of condensing the steam and pumping it back into the system for reuse—the step where most of the heat energy is lost—the turbine is linked to an axle that in turn spins the generator. The literature on this topic now states without explanation that "the generator uses the kinetic energy from the turbine to make electricity." Lovely, and no doubt true, but still unclear. How fast would I have to crank my ice cream machine for the same thing to happen?

Do it fast enough with a turbine and the generator creates powerful electrical energy. That is occurring

Part Two: Feeding the Cats

at a grand scale in the turbine electrical generators at the power plant. The engineering? The amount of wire? The insulating systems, energy to turn the rotors, gear the shafts, and move the current through the stator and out into the transmission lines. Heat is the main waste product, but so are the gases released by burning coal and gas. Newer innovations like solar photovoltaic cells don't use turbines, but the quantity of energy they generate is still small by contrast to that of turbines.

Once generated, the electricity can travel to a transformer where the voltage is increased by moving the current between two coils with different ratios of "windings" or turns. This physical structure creates a differential that can be controlled. The minds that manage the electrical grid need to be cognizant of loads, demands, fluctuations in use patterns, and hazards from storms and fires. Work on a transmission line is highly skilled and often dangerous. Line workers, service employees, surveyors, and staff engineers working as ground men, on utility line clearance, and other maintenance and repair operations are all in high demand. The construction of the "line and pole" systems also has to be rodent proof. With their belts, boots, and hardhats, bright safety vests and blue jeans, the crews that restore power in an outage and brave the elements keep homes, hospitals, and businesses supplied.

More, much more, could be said of each stage along

the way from power plant to home, but for now, just a few words on the home electrical system. The point at which electricity enters the house or institution is called a service drop.[119] Here the meter box gets connected to the breaker box as a safety mechanism before the current goes through the wires to outlets. Voltage regulators and lightning arresters as well as other essential parts of the system, each with their own manufacturing history, are also part of the infrastructure. A simple search on "lightning arresters" takes us down another rabbit hole and then another until we are in the work of "impedance" and "travelling waves" that "spark over prefixed voltage" and other descriptions of the operation of these essential units.

Enough. Finish here with the switch on my kitchen light in the morning and the physical mechanism that either opens or closes contacts to allow current to flow. This is made of corrosion-resistant metal. The bulbs of the track lighting system above the counters are screwed into the fitting so they connect with the metal contacts. A thin metal filament is suspended in the glass tube, itself filled with an inert gas. When the current goes through the bulb, the electrons knock into the atoms of the metal filament and cause them to vibrate. We are in the realm of bumper cars, it seems. Vibrating electrons get charged in the process, and then fall back to lower energy levels, releasing energy as photons, or light. A common metal for filaments is tungsten stretched incredibly thin and also coiled. In a traditional 60-watt bulb, the filament was about two and a half feet long but coiled into a form less than an inch. Metal, inert gas, and a completely sealed oxygen-free chamber that is a near-vacuum keepß the tungsten from evaporating. And the ecological costs of making the lightbulbs? And mining the tungsten? Making the glass? Fabricating the wires and the switches and switch-plates? And of course now they are mainly LED bulbs, so cycle back to that section of the coffee maker and its lights for a tale of sandwiched materials and light emissions.

I will leave this to you to imagine. Investigating every single bit of the material in every part of these systems leads into similarly elaborate networks that eventually trace a connection between the earth as a resource and human consumption with exhalation of toxins, wastes, gases, and other forms of affluvia all along the way.

I have come to the end of this description of making coffee and feeding the cats.

Afterword: Out the door

As I leave the house the sun is just edging over the hills to the east, tinting the sky. For a few moments I am aware of the geography, of living in a basin rimmed by mountains that stretches west to the Pacific. Then the scene on the street overwhelms me. The brand makes of cars parked against the curbs and in the driveways have shifted in the last decade from Toyotas and Hondas to Teslas and Porches, an occasional Maserati, with lots of BMWs and Mercedes in the mix. Most self-consciously parked for display, the hybrids flaunt their ecological correctness. Their shining surface of baked enamel paint finish shines in the early light, concealing the metal frame. High hard rubber tires, threaded with a web of steel mesh, held tight with long bolts behind the cover of the hubcaps, each have their small nozzle through which to receive pressurized air. Many details of chrome insignia dot the car body. The cast plastic-rubber bumpers are designed to resist impact. The windows contain wires to defog and defrost, with handle mechanisms connected to a small motor, lock devices, and wipers made to size specifications and blades in a variety of sizes and shapes. Each and every feature of the cars is part of a long line of industrial and manufacturing techniques. The supply chains stretch back into the earth, the processes pour pollution into the air, earth, and water. The trail of human casualties and costs strews the path to final products with a litter of wasted lives and opportunities. And the upholstery? And the radio and all of the many interior features, these too are entangled in a mass of interconnected activities. Each automobile contains more electronics and computational capacity than was used in the first Moon landing. My mind races.

I cannot look at anything without seeing all of the supply chains and processes through which it came into being from raw materials to finished products consumed and then discarded.

Beyond the cars, the houses are in various states of renovation or construction. Demolition equipment is everywhere, plowing the old wood frame bungalows into a pile of rubble to be replaced by bunker-like structures of concrete, rebar, and glass. The modest family houses of the 1940s and 50s are bulldozed daily, their lots filled to the property line with dwellings that are more than twice their volume, and have five or more bedrooms, baths, family rooms and finished basements, pools and porches, patios and home entertainment centers. The interiors of new construction are finished in somewhat sustainable wood, stone quarried around the globe, cut, polished, and finished elsewhere. All of the stuff of the world is available inventory—hardwood and softwood, bamboo and oak, pine and redwood, ceramic and marble, along with all of the composites produced with resins and plastics. The houses are sealed tight for thermal insulation and control by a so-called smart system that uses electronic feedback loops to regulate the temperature and humidity. The polished metal appliances with their own elaborate electronic systems dependent on chips and circuits, are living on electricity. The refrigerator is stocked, so is the pantry, with packaged and processed foodstuffs, fresh vegetables and fruits newly delivered through a network of transportation and shipping that creates easy availability of goods from throughout the globe. Mexican avocados, Spanish blood oranges, mangoes from Costa Rica and olives from Greece can be had in the local supermarket where the management of constant flows of abundance create their own stockpiles of waste and challenges for inventory management. Behind every door on the street are rooms with televisions and cell phones, cable connections and multiple devices, at least one or two for every member of the family and then some. The pets (not mine) have chips embedded in their skin, part of another elaborate system of information and registry that enables tracking. They, too, have their beds and blanket accessories for sleeping, playing, walking, eating, and grooming.

Waste abounds. We produce trash at a rate that far outstrips any capacity to deal with it properly. Solid waste management—nice term, but a stand-in for gross negligence. According to the blogsite dumpsters.com, Americans produce 4.5 pounds of trash a day, about three times as much per person as the average in the rest of the world.[119] The break-down by waste type shows food, plastics, and paper leading the list. Landfills receive about 140 million tons of waste a year. Packaging is more than a quarter of this—all that stupid shiny plastic, vacu-formed and impossible to open, holding a toy, a battery, a small item of hardware or electronics. Amazon alone ships over 600 million packages a year in cardboard boxes. Think about it. 5,000 tons is the equivalent of 10 jumbo jets so the landfills in the United States are receiving the equivalent of 28,000 jumbo jets a year in volume.[120] Staggering to imagine. While all kinds of solutions are proposed and possible, the endless-seeming flow continues.[121] Lack of regulation, and low motivation, little return on the obvious investment to re-use, a complete disregard for the extent to which all of this has impacts above and beyond the mere accumulation of massive amounts of unusable stuff—these are all contributing factors. But perhaps above all there is the ease of consumption, at least within the mainstream of American culture and its increasing desire for grab-and-go immediate gratification.

My morning run fills me with sadness and despair, seeing the scale at which consumption occurs. And I feel my spirit collapse, realizing that every aspect of this routine implicates me in systems of abuse, exploitation, and damage. To understand those systems in all their complexity is overwhelming. How am I to intervene in the processes by which the coffee bag is made, the grinder produced, the cat food created, the labels printed, the pigments processed, the cardboard printed, formed, and cut, the single-use plastics molded and the very bins themselves pressed from pellets into strong bold colorful shapes?

If I recover the lifecycle of these processes, by what set of metrics can I assign a cost to each? Carbon footprint and fossil fuels are only one slice of the whole measure that needs to be applied. And every object in my life, on my work table, kitchen counter, closest and drawers is part of this vast system of made-ness by which we have inured ourselves to the scale of production and consumption that normalizes itself in affluent societies. North American super markets have a more abundant supply and range of food than the wealthiest individuals would have had two hundred years ago. All-year supplies of strawberries, citrus, and exotic fruits, meat of every variety slaughtered and sold fresh, fish, vegetables, fragile produce and robust dairy products are available in seemingly endless supply. Single use packaging for one meal's worth of spinach, pre-chopped salad or soup ingredients, and bottled drinks. Everywhere, in every aisle in every store in every neighborhood in every small and large community in America, the packaging—plastic form-molded, containing more plastic items—pink figurines, blue action heros, little animals of synthetic ingredients, a world of unnecessary objects, many for children, but not all. Batteries and cosmetics, hygiene products and all of the dross of daily life come contained in these little barrier cells of transparent plastic. And almost all of it is stuff no one needs, not even remotely, manufactured simply to stimulate the desire for acquisition which it provokes upon display.

Production of plastics creates about 6% of current (2021) global greenhouse gasses. We need to reduce the carbon dioxide emitted when burned in recycling. Every water source on the planet is permeated with microplastics. Global warming is aggravated by the gasses released in plastic manufacturing. The holy grail of net-zero-emission hangs like a mechanical rabbit in front of a race for survival.

Insidious pollution
The yards are overflowing with plants, patches of lawn, watering systems on automatic timers, their spraying heads connected to copper pipes designed to deliver moisture in a controlled way. The sidewalks are concrete, and, like the curbs, were poured in forms of wood, long gone, from enormous trucks that mixed the paste and delivered it on site. The surfaces of the streets are refreshed on a regular basis, recoated with an asphalt slurry, black and tacky, rolled out smoothly until it meets the curbs though the dark gravel frays at the edge like an unfinished pie dough. The trash bins and recycling containers are filled

to bursting, their connection to the daily flow of delivery trucks easily legible in the Amazon, FedEx, and UPS labels.

The patio furniture made of recycled plastic and wood furniture seems so clearly the eco-friendly thing. But the literal off-gassing from these products produces a form of volatile organic compound that is carcinogenic. Better to buy the floor model, which had already exhaled a good portion of its toxins into the store showroom. Warm and humid conditions aid in off-gassing, increasing release of VOCs. Volatile organic compounds are major sources of ground-water contamination.[122] Paint and lacquer, cleaning supplies, copiers, printers, pesticides, cleaning supplies, glue and adhesives, markers, correction fluids. The cleaning routines of degreasing and disinfecting release VOCs. Paints and wax—contain organic solvents, so do most cleaning materials. Vinyl flooring. Air fresheners. Cosmetics. Fuel oil. Dry cleaning. Photocopiers and printers.

Think of everything that is airborne. Particles of all kinds move through the atmosphere, carried on wind and mixed with rain, present in clouds and smoke, deposited on surfaces, stratified and turned into a natural archive legible as a record of past events. Even out of doors, a perfume trail or scent of body odor lingers in passing, the evidence of molecules of something carried on the air. Inside an enclosed structure, a house or school, the smell of food, cleaners, mildew, unwashed clothing or fresh soap disperse throughout the space. In a religious structure, the smell of incense or candlewax scents the air. And the aftermath of fire leaves ash deposits in which we can write our names, as does the residue of volcanic eruption. Unseen and deeply toxic, carbon monoxide, a deadly odorless presence, replaces oxygen in the blood and leads to death. Radon, naturally occurring but radioactive, is the second leading cause of lung cancer in the United States after tobacco smoke, a conspicuous and more deadly pollutant. Lead and mercury, accumulating in our organs, teeth, and bones are difficult to detect in water and food. No smoke alarm rings when you are served a portion of fish with a toxic level of heavy metal. Extend these images to include the pollutants that affect whole communities and populations. Water in Flint, Michigan, Black Soot in Port Harcourt, Nigeria, the toxic gas that exposed half a million people to contamination in Bhopal, India in 1984 are all disasters at massive scale. They are also all effects of affluence, created as the side-effect of deregulated industrial processes that are part of systemic social injustice baked into contemporary activity. Ecological disaster is social disaster brought on by political inertia and ethical negligence.

To say that affluvia is the toxic-offgassing of affluence is not merely to state a metaphor, but a fact—literally and actually many airborne pollutants are produced by the practices that make "ordinary, every day life" what it is. Think about it. A car. A television. A phone. These are the things of daily life for many people. If there is approximately 1 car for every 5 people on earth, with a disproportionate number of these concentrated in the global North and West, what are the costs of manufacture, as well as operation, of these vehicles. The affluent tend to think in terms of controlling emissions. This leaves out the lifecycle of production with its many streams of toxic waste, metals, battery production, and energy consumption. Estimates are that seventy-five percent of the world's population has a phone. Eighty-nine percent of homes in the world have a television. But only seventy-one percent has clean drinking water and about seventy-four have basic sanitation facilities. Needless to say, the concentration of advantage maps onto longstanding patterns of global inequity, colonialism, extraction industries, and political asymmetry in relation to control of the environment and local resources.

Above the street the electrical wires connect poles to boxes, an elaborate and vulnerable seeming mesh of exposed infrastructure, its insulating coatings and hardware fittings a kludged-seeming collection of past and present infrastructure. Below the street, the gas lines and sewers, water mains and pipes, all having to serve to support the new growth as well as the old. The dependence on all of this invisible architecture is terrifying to contemplate. And as I run, trucks rumble through the still-sleeping neighborhood, bringing construction supplies, stacks of lumber, palettes of sheetrock, bags of concrete, and piles of stone are all being offloaded while the rubbish and rubble in the bins mounts high above the rims. A runner moves through the streets, shoes cushioned with a carefully engineered architecture of support for arches and heels, tied with laces woven and braided, ends finished with tight plastic caps, threaded through eyelets attached to the fabric and leather. A monogram for the branding shines with reflective metallic detail, and the colors of the shoes are the result of elaborate chemical procedures combined with pigments gleaned from the resources of the earth. They are wearing earbuds, blue-tooth connected to their iPhone, listening to a podcast recorded weeks ago and stored in a file on the cloud which they can access directly this morning on a device that depends on technologies that connect all corners of the globe.

The phone is powered by a lithium battery. Lithium, a lightweight metal, perfect for batteries, except for its volatile temperament. It is highly reactive, imagine, and this because its valence electron gets loaned easily to any reaction in its vicinity. Like a bad pup that can't be trusted to interact with other dogs or a wayward teen inclined to pick a fight, that electron is in a loose outer orbit that is hard to control. More so when we realize that "electron" is a metaphor for a bit of negative charge at the outer edges of its own small atomic universe.

And if I drop my phone and break it open and a fragment of the lithium comes into contact with water it explodes. But meanwhile, the rare desert wildflower, Tiehm's buckwheat, is threatened with extinction on a site in Arizona where an Australian company is trying to open a lithium mine. Leave aside the diplomatic and trade deal complexities of this, the regulations that have to be examined, ignored, supported or suppressed. Keep in mind just the timely connection between a mining operation and a high desert area that is threatened with development of roads and rampant habitat destruction. The drive for lithium has kept the company persistent in its bid to make a deal with the Bureau of Land Management so that it can extract the precious metal and process it for target industries like the manufacture of electric cars.

And this is nothing, this is just the beginning of the day, the smallest of moments between waking and starting into the routines of daily life. I cannot fathom the complexity of these connections, and everything I see, from the smallest cast off bottle cap and bit of plastic detritus to the billboard glowing in the skyline miles away spins out into a mass of interrelated pathways and processes. My mind reels at the made-ness of the world. My heart breaks with sadness at the waste of the precious beauty of the earth. We could have done all of this differently. We still could.

● ●

Conclusion

First World consumers already know we are participating in monstrous global systems of inequity, injustice, and other forms of unevenly distributed privilege, hardship, and misery through the path dependencies and infrastructure lifecycles that we rely on and take fully for granted.

Every day the off-gassing intensifies. A simple stroll through my neighborhood provides ample evidence. The detritus generated by each purchase accumulates. The recycle bin overflows. The sheer mass of cardboard alone buries the future in trash. We mortgage the air, our water, the legacy of earth with no hope, or plan, of how to repay the debt of permanently lost resources. None of this is a surprise. But on we go, in our familiar patterns, ignoring the realities of production, the extraction industries, the human toll and political upheaval wrought by the path dependencies in which supply lines function. A sick syndrome produces exhaustion. A huge passivity vortex sustains inertia, inaction, a collective psychic entropy moving inexorably towards collapse. Meanwhile, the replication of behavior continues in a cycle of transmission so effectively addicting it hardly stops for sleep or air. The very fact of doom is so familiar it long ago ceased to register, especially as the scale increases to the point of incomprehensible effects.

Affluvia is more than the sum of these effects, it is a generating force within the damned and dying system. We are active agents as well as instrumental subjects of the force, submissive by virtue of the self-delusion that commands us.

What we need is a Blueprint for Otherwise. Imagine, waking to a quiet world, without light pollution or noise, and only the sounds of birds, insects, living creatures, the stirring of wind in leaves. Energy supplied from solar panels, geothermal sources, locally sourced. Work patterns mapped onto bike, pedestrian, and mass-transit systems. Recycled materials so expertly refashioned extraction could slow to a trickle. A status quo of sustainability, in which growth and progress are managed to keep ecological systems balanced. A global equity system in which distribution of benefits and wealth preserves local customs while allowing equal access to food, water, education, medicine, and a holistic lifestyle. Music, dance, arts and crafts, care work within communities, urban gardening, maintenance of the systems that support us are integrated into daily life and routines. A peaceable kingdom rooted in social justice, environmental equity, genuine commitment to a world without exploitation or pollution. Possible? Yes. Probable? Up to us.

AFFLUVIA

End Notes

[1]https://dailycoffeenews.com/2013/07/17/farmworkers-left-behind-the-human-cost-of-coffee-production/

[2]https://dailycoffeenews.com/2013/07/17/farmworkers-left-behind-the-human-cost-of-coffee-production/

[3]http://www.coffeehabitat.com/2008/10/fight-poverty-quit-drinking-corporate-coffee/

[4]https://www.globallivingwage.org/

[5]https://www.numbeo.com/cost-of-living/country_result.jsp?country=Guatemala

[6]Bristol University, Department of Chemistry, "Endosulfan," (Accessed 1/18/2022) http://www.chm.bris.ac.uk/motm/endosulfan/endosulfanh.htm

[7]Socio-economic Conditions of Women Workers in

Plantation Industry, 2008-09, Government of India, Ministry of Labour & Employment, Labour Bureau, Chandigarh http://www.labourbureaunew.gov.in/UserContent/SECOWW_Plantation_200809.pdf

[8]The Coffee Roasting Company, https://www.tcrc.coffee/products-1/Roastingplants

[9]Perfect Daily Grind, March 18, 2021; https://perfectdailygrind.com/2021/03/exploring-the-environmental-impact-of-coffee-roasting/

[10]Improving the living and working conditions in the Brazilian coffee-producing sector Global Coffee Platform. https://www.globalcoffeeplatform.org/collective-action-initiatives/2020/improvement-of-living-and-working-conditions/

[11]https://wkaiglobal.com/blogs/how-pet-plastic-is-made-from-raw-materials-to-recyclable-containers

[12]https://www3.epa.gov/ttnchie1/ap42/ch06/final/c06s06-2.pdf

[13]https://pubs.rsc.org/en/content/articlelanding/2019/gc/c8gc03666g#!

[14]https://www.smartproducts.com/

[15] Thomas Thwaites, How I made a toaster from scratch, https://www.youtube.com/watch?v=5ODzO7Lz_pw&ab_channel=TED

[16] https://www.worldometers.info/coal/

[17] https://www3.epa.gov/ttnchie1/old/ap42/ch12/s02/final/c12s02_1995.pdf

[18] https://www.jaha.org/edu/discovery_center/work/img/conditions/

[19] https://www.cdc.gov/niosh/topics/metalworking/default.html

[20] https://cadenceblades.com/

[21] https://verite.org/wp-content/uploads/2016/11/Research-on-Working-Conditions-in-the-Liberia-Rubber-Sector__9.16.pdf

[22] https://acadiantextiles.com/the-environmental-impact-of-polyethylene-and-polypropylene/

[23] https://www.sentryair.com/blog/industry-applications/plastics/the-hazards-of-plastic-injection-molding-recommended-engineering-safety-controls/

[24] https://polymer-additives.specialchem.com/selection-guide/pigments-for-plastics

[25] https://englishrussia.com/2012/08/10/how-power-cords-are-made/

[26] https://www.greenpeace.org/usa/wp-content/uploads/legacy/Global/usa/report/2009/4/pvc-the-poison-plastic.html

[27] https://www.thomasnet.com/articles/top-suppliers/pvc-manufacturers-suppliers/

[28] Sources consulted for this section:
https://www.environmentalpollution.in/pollution/steel-industry-pollution/how-to-control-pollution-in-iron-and-steel-industry/7000

https://www.iup.edu/library/departments/archives/coal/mining-history/history-of-coke.html

https://ourworldindata.org/fertilizers

https://wiki.ece.cmu.edu/ddl/index.php/Coffee_grinder

https://laborrights.org/sites/default/files/publications-and-resources/UNMIL_enviro_report.pdf

https://www.ukessays.com/essays/archaeology/iron-smelting-technology.php

https://www.ftmsino.com/blog/

how-is-the-iron-ore-mined/
https://www.rubbercal.com/industrial-rubber/history-of-rubber/
https://www.coruba.co.uk/blog/synthetic-rubber-manufacturing-process/

[29]https://twosidesna.org/US/paper-grows-trees-quite-fast/
https://pr.princeton.edu/news/04/q3/0927-trees.htm

[30]Ju Wu, et al., "Biogenic volatile organic compounds in forest therapy base: A source of pollutants or a therapy base?" Science of the Total Environment, Volume 931, 25 June 2024, 172944. https://www.sciencedirect.com/science/article/abs/pii/S0048969724030912

[31]https://paperontherocks.com/2019/03/22/water-waste-paper-industry-what-makes-pulp-paper-production-thirsty-business/

[32]https://majestycoffee.com/blogs/posts/bleached-vs-unbleached-coffee-filters

[33]https://www.theworldcounts.com/stories/Environmental_Impact_of_Paper_Production

[34]Matthew Hall, Mining Technology, https://www.mining-technology.com/analysis/six-things-sand-mining/

[35]Desert Sand vs. Beach Sand: Understanding the Differences

https://sand-boarding.com/desert-sand-vs-beach-sand/

[36]https://project.geo.msu.edu/geogmich/sand.html

[37]911 Metalurgist, "Silica Sand Processing and Sand Washing Equipment," https://www.911metalurgist.com/blog/silica-sand-processing-sand-washing-plant-equipment

[38]https://www.o-i.com/our-story/how-glass-bottles-and-jars-are-made/

[39]https://aluminiumleader.com/production/how_aluminium_is_produced/

[40]https://aluminiumleader.com/production/how_aluminium_is_produced/

[41]https://www.zotefoams.com/about-us/

[42]https://www.researchgate.net/publication/269539028_Extend_of_arsenic_contamination_and_its_impact_on_food_chain_and_human_health_in_Eastern_Ganges_Basin_A_Review/figures?lo=1

[43]https://en.wikipedia.org/wiki/Phosphor#White_LEDs

[44]https://patents.google.com/patent/CN2768052Y/en

[45]Stu Wøstu, Ham Radio School, https://www.hamradio-school.com/post/liquid-crystal-displays

[46]https://www.circuitstoday.com/invention-history-of-liquid-crystal-display-lcd

[47]https://www.physlink.com/education/askexperts/ae303.cfm

[48]http://www.madehow.com/Volume-1/Liquid-Crystal-Display-LCD.html

[49]https://docs.microsoft.com/en-us/typography/font-list/lcd   https://www.fontspace.com/category/lcd
[50]https://www.fontspace.com/digital-7-font-f7087

[51]https://bestengineeringprojects.com/programmable-timer/

[52]https://www.utmel.com/blog/categories/integrated%20circuit/what-is-a-digital-integrated-circuit-and-how-do-we-use-it

[53]https://www.ncbi.nlm.nih.gov/pmc/articles/PMC8390110/

[54]Bacteria and lithium.

[55]National Center for Biology Information, NIH 10.3402/

ehtj.v4i0.7110

[56] https://home.howstuffworks.com/coffee-maker.htm

[57] https://en.wikipedia.org/wiki/Thermal_paste

[58] James Clerk Maxwell, Theory of Heat (London: Longmans Green and Co., 1871), 7 (as per the Wiki citation https://en.wikipedia.org/wiki/Heat#cite_note-24).

[59] https://continentalsteel.com/nickel-alloys/

[60] https://www.reuters.com/article/uk-china-worker/insight-young-chinese-workers-seek-end-to-eating-bitterness-idUSBRE83504Q20120406

[61] https://www.livescience.com/19654-beep-digital-sounds-annoying.html

[62] https://extension.psu.edu/carbon-methane-emissions-and-the-dairy-cow#:~:text=Methane%20Production%20and%20the%20Dairy,the%20total%20CH4%20emitted.

[63] https://extension.psu.edu/dairy-sense-keeping-the-dairy-right-sized

[64] https://www.youtube.com/watch?v=psXO83vFU7k

[65] https://www.ncbi.nlm.nih.gov/pmc/articles/PMC6792142/

[66] https://beyondpesticides.org/dailynewsblog/2020/07/from-udder-to-table-toxic-pesticides-found-in-conventional-milk-not-organic-milk/

[67] https://www.beyondpesticides.org/resources/pesticide-gateway?pesticideid=24

[68] https://mercyforanimals.org/

[69] https://www.theguardian.com/environment/2022/aug/16/most-damaging-farm-products-organic-pasture-fed-beef-lamb

[70] https://www.researchgate.net/figure/Typical-Fourdrinier-forming-section-on-a-paper-machine-See-Acknowledgements-for-figure_fig1_313889989

[71] http://www.madehow.com/Volume-4/Milk-Carton.html

[72] https://www.usgs.gov/centers/national-minerals-information-center/clays-statistics-and-information

[73] https://www.alliedmarketresearch.com/refractory-material-market-A14896

[74] https://www.911metallurgist.com/blog/beneficiation-process-kaolin-clay

[75] https://www.911metallurgist.com/blog/beneficiation-process-kaolin-clay

[76] https://response-avoid.com/qa/what-kind-of-clay-is-used-for-mugs-2.html

[77] S. Ramanaiah and Y.V. Sanjay Das, "Environmental Impact Assessment of Quartz and Feldspar Mining in Kamareddy District, Telangana State, South India," Journal of Information and Computational Science, Vol. 9, 11 (2019), 755-768. http://www.joics.org/gallery/ics-1717.pdf

[78] https://www.thepolishedplate.com/philippe-deshoulieres-m54.aspx

[79] https://alexanders.com/blog/a-very-brief-history-of-cmyk/

[80] https://www.tonerbuzz.com/blog/all-about-printer-ink-everything-you-need-to-know

[81] https://www.pcimag.com/articles/85040-pigments-in-ink

[82] https://www.pcimag.com/articles/85040-pigments-in-ink

[83] http://printwiki.org/Pigment

[84] https://www.epa.gov/sites/default/files/2020-10/documents/c06s01.pdf "Organic Chemical Process Industry"

[85] https://en.wikipedia.org/wiki/Quenching_(fluorescence)

[86] https://www.epa.gov/eg/carbon-black-manufacturing-effluent-guidelines

[87] https://www.epa.gov/sites/default/files/2018-06/documents/carbon-black-mfg_final_43-fr-1343_01-09-1978.pdf

[88] https://www.color.org/v4_prmg.xalter

[89] Nisha Chawla, September 18, 2021, Business Khabar, https://www.businesskhabar.com/money/stock-tips-the-rising-prices-of-aluminum-will-give-wings-to-the-shares-of-this-company-know-how-much-profit-is-expected/

[90] https://www3.epa.gov/ttn/chief/ap42/ch09/final/c9s05-3.pdf

[91] http://www.madehow.com/Volume-7/Pyrex.html

[92] https://www.aga.org/natural-gas/delivery/how-does-the-natural-gas-delivery-system-work-/

[93] https://www.scienceworld.ca/resource/wonderful-water/

[94] https://www.americangeosciences.org/education/k5geosource/content/water/why-is-water-special

[95] https://www.watereducation.org/aquapedia/los-angeles-aqueduct-and-owens-valley

[96] https://en.wikipedia.org/wiki/Los_Angeles_Aqueduct#/media/File:Shangri-La_Estates.png

[97] https://betterbuildingssolutioncenter.energy.gov/showcase-projects/los-angeles-department-water-and-power-los-angeles-aqueduct-filtration-plant

[98] https://www.npr.org/2016/04/14/473806134/how-do-we-get-our-drinking-water-in-the-u-s

[99] https://www.watereducation.org/post/how-drinking-water-treated

[100] https://www.wonderopolis.org/wonder/how-does-water-get-to-my-faucet

[101] https://synergist.aiha.org/protecting-wastewater-treatment-workers

[102] https://synergist.aiha.org/protecting-wastewater-treatment-workers

[103] https://en.wikipedia.org/wiki/Hyperion_sewage_treatment_plant

[104] https://www.lacitysan.org/san/faces/home

[105] https://www.drcdinc.com/projects-blog/

End Notes 327

copy-of-hyperion-wastewater-treatment-plant-solids-handling-facility-digester-expansion-project-city-of-los-angeles

[106]https://en.wikipedia.org/wiki/Hyperion_sewage_treatment_plant

[107]http://koordinates-tiles-b.global.ssl.fastly.net/services/tiles/v4/thumbnail/layer=98169.306789,style=auto/1200x630.png

[108]https://www.lacitysan.org/san/faces/home/portal/s-lsh-wwd/s-lsh-wwd-cw/s-lsh-wwd-cw-p/s-lsh-wwd-cw-p-tp?_adf.ctrl-state=16ryk97dzc_5&_afrLoop=13191177560967745#!

[109]https://bacteriadirect.com/bacteria-wastewater-treatment/?msclkid=b1265ee1657b1ab10a9c3def2f112626

[110]https://bacteriadirect.com/industries/municipal-treatment-plant/

[111]https://www.lacitysan.org/san/faces/home/portal/s-lsh-wwd/s-lsh-wwd-cw/s-lsh-wwd-cw-p/s-lsh-wwd-cw-p-tp?_adf.ctrl-state=16ryk97dzc_5&_afrLoop=13191177560967745#!

[112]https://wonders.physics.wisc.edu/what-is-electricity/

[113]https://wonders.physics.wisc.edu/what-is-electricity/

[114] https://www.eia.gov/energyexplained/electricity/the-science-of-electricity.php

[115] https://www.eia.gov/energyexplained/electricity/

[116] https://www.ab-sessions-plumbing-building-services.com/where-does-los-angeles-get-its-electricity/

[117] https://www.explainthatstuff.com/powerplants.html

[118] https://www.explainthatstuff.com/powerplants.html

[119] https://caec.coop/electric-service/how-power-is-delivered-to-your-home/

[120] https://www.dumpsters.com/blog/us-trash-production

[121] https://oceanconservancy.org/blog/2013/05/14/what-does-10-million-pounds-of-trash-look-like/

[122] https://upstreamsolutions.org/

[123] https://www.epa.gov/indoor-air-quality-iaq/what-are-volatile-organic-compounds-vocs

End Notes

AFFLUVIA

www.ingramcontent.com/pod-product-compliance
Lightning Source LLC
Chambersburg PA
CBHW052127030426
42337CB00028B/5054